# Survival Guide to Professional Exams

**Preparation Tips to Ace the Test!**

# Michael Africk

BENTLEY PRESS

Survival Guide to Professional Exams
Preparation Tips to Ace the Test!

Copyright © 1994 by Michael Africk.

ISBN Number 0-9641093-6-0

Library of Congress Catalog Card Number: 94-71321

*for my wife, Cynthia*

# Survival Guide to Professional Exams
## Preparation Tips to Ace the Test!

# CONTENTS

# Introduction

*"It has become increasingly clear that examinations of all sorts are relied on now more than ever."*

You have heard the phrase often enough; someone claims that no matter how well he or she knows the material to be tested, they just do not "test well." As a result, their performance on a given exam does not accurately reflect their abilities or understanding of the subject matter. Rather, what *is* reflected is the level of distraction which prevented peak performance. On the other hand, we have probably all had the experience in academia in which an academic result is achieved without much effort. For example, you did not study as much or as comparatively speaking, as well, as you may have on other occasions, only to be surprised by a grade or a test score well above your expectations. The central question, then, is what marks the difference? The answer: your approach to the material to be mastered, both before and during the exam.

It has become increasingly clear that examinations of all sorts are relied on now more than ever. As we progress in our professional pursuits, the examinations get more specialized and have a much larger impact. Take the legal profession, for example. After surviving a grueling day of multiple choice testing called the LSAT just to get *in* to law school, and countless midterm and final examinations during three years of graduate work, each lawyer is required to pass a state bar examination. Depending on the state, that exam can be anywhere from two days of essays and multiple choice questions, to four days of such testing. It can also include special "performance" sections requiring detailed analysis of complex fact patterns in a short amount of time. To do well, one has to review vast amounts of material before the exam and wisely allocate time to the various sections on exam day. It is just as much a test of pre-examination *study management* as it is an endurance test to get through it all! The faint of heart just fall by the waste side.

The CPA examination is just as grueling, involving accounting, auditing, business law and other subjects which must be mastered in one test taking session. Real estate agents and brokers all have to pass their respective examinations to gain the coveted license which allows them to earn a living. Teachers take qualifying exams to earn their credential, as do stock brokers, foreign and civil service candidates and nurses — these are just a sampling of the literally hundreds of job categories out there requiring qualifying exams.

Need I go on? What test are you preparing for? Could you conceivably practice your profession without taking and passing it? The list of tests out there and the requirement that they be satisfactorily completed before a person is deemed qualified is indeed long. Any profession today requires some proof of training and ability, and increasingly, the demonstration comes in the form of a passing grade on a test.

On the importance of test taking and test passing, circumstantial evidence abounds. Take, for example, the fact that exam prep courses are a *multi-million* dollar industry, almost to the point that enrolling in such a course is viewed by some test takers as merely a way to effectively neutralize the advantage of the peer who has already signed up. For some exams, taking a prep course seems like a prerequisite to passing! For several reasons, these courses are indeed valuable, as we will discuss later, but their value is limited because they generally do not stress how to manage your studies and the other aspects of your life during the preparation period. This book does that, and is meant to supplement the nuts and bolts found in study aids, books and courses. Your test preparation will be greatly enhanced by the suggestions in approach contained in this book.

This book is written from experience, and is meant to be a primer on test preparation and study management. It is full of tips and approaches and discussions of techniques to help you perform your best *prior to* the exam *and* on examination day. This book is written for the legion of test takers each year, who, having chosen a profession, must master a professional exam to advance their careers. Use this book as a guide before you embark on your test preparation and refer to it often during your preparation period. It will help you maximize the time and energy you devote to the discipline of passing your professional exam.

# 1

# Understanding the Role of Professional Exams

*"The advent of professional exams stemmed from two basic needs: the need to protect the public from unscrupulous and unqualified people, and the need to further differentiate among and between qualified candidates when evaluating them for admission to educational programs."*

Anyone who has geared up to take a professional exam will readily admit that as a whole, the experience is arduous and nerve racking. The pressure revolves around the fact that these tests, due largely to their formats, emphasize and reward a student's short term memory on exam day. They draw largely on a student's stamina and grace under pressure.

We can debate whether testing those attributes is a valuable pursuit, but in the meantime, we should acknowledge certain realities: the undeniable nature of the professional exam is that it is generally objective and impersonal. It does

11

not pretend to measure character traits or professional expertise in the same way that workplace performance evaluations do, or yearly course grades might. The test score has no component showing such valuable work attributes as reliability, integrity, leadership or improvement over the long term, just as it does not measure professional experience or competence. It just shows how you tested on certain material, on a given day, and that's all.

Sometimes the material tested seems so unrelated to the underlying profession that one really wonders what value the score has. For example, the LSAT has a whole section on logic games, requiring the student to solve, under time pressures, a series of logic brain teasers. Test makers claim that good performance on this section bodes well for law school course performance because the law is, after all, logical. Interesting premise, don't you think?

Fortunately, the bar exam that students must pass years later in order to practice law comes closer to testing what would seem a more relevant mark — knowledge of the law — with its essay questions requiring legal analysis. But on the same test, students must also master multiple choice questions, a rather curious way to test legal scholarship. After all, when was the last time a client went to an attorney with a legal problem, asked the attorney which one among four alternative answers was right, and expected the correct answer in less than 1.7 minutes (that's the prorated allocation of time for each multiple choice question on a typical state bar exam)? Not recently.

Understanding the history and role of the professional exam goes a long way in placing your preparation efforts in the proper perspective.

Professional examinations are a relatively new phenomenon. Indeed, there are actually college graduates among us who never took the SAT to get into college. That test was introduced in the late 1920's and came into universal prominence in the late 1950's. Likewise, there are some practicing doctors who did not suffer through an MCAT. A century ago, it was quite routine to train for a career in law by serving as a legal apprentice — no formal exam required; after a fixed amount of time, and upon the recommendation of a practicing attorney, the candidate gained full fledged admission to the state bar. In an effort to protect the public, qualifying tests for real estate brokers and salespersons were established around the turn of this century. Prior to that, a land dealer simply had to register his sales office with local authorities, but did not have to pass a qualifying exam.

The advent of professional exams stemmed from two basic needs: the need to protect the public from unscrupulous and unqualified people, and the need to further differentiate among and between qualified candidates when evaluating them for admission to educational programs. If the purpose of the professional exam you are taking is rooted in "public protection" policy, a passing grade on the exam is usually all that is required. What is considered "passing" may be subject to interpretation by current members of the profession (in an effort to control the number of practitioners in the field and maintain an operative monopoly), but a passing score is nevertheless all that is required. In that case, the candidate receives word that he or she passed, but the score itself is not applied to any further purpose. An unsuccessful candidate, however, usually receives a breakdown of the failing score, in order to substantiate the failure and assist the candidate in addressing deficient areas before again attempting to pass the test.

If, on the other hand, the test grew out of a need to differentiate candidate A from candidate B for purposes of admission to an educational program, the emphasis is on an actual score — and the higher the better. With these types of professional exams, the score is a surrogate for the old fashion personal introduction or letter of recommendation prepared by a respected practitioner. Today, a high score will grab the attention of an admissions committee in the same way that a personal introduction or prestigious letter of recommendation might have done in years past.

In a way, the evolution of personal referrals into objective scoring is a positive development, because the former system was fraught with inequities. Naturally, it was based on who you knew and how well you knew them and what pull they had. With the present test requirement, the emphasis shifts to *what* you know and to how good you are at *showing* what you know. These attributes seem a little more relevant to sizing up a candidate.

One may argue that even the present system of test taking is fraught with inequities, but its better than the former system of introductions. Besides, presently, its the best one we've got. But debating the good or evil nature of these exams is beyond the scope of this book. The fact is that professional tests are here to stay, that you are reading this book because you have to ace one in the near future, and that you are going to give it your all to do just that.

One thing is clear. These tests may open doors, but they have very little relevance to career success. They do not measure the character traits that the professional must exhibit every day to earn the public's trust and dollars and thus succeed in the market place. For the most part, they do not measure professional expertise, either, evidenced by the fact that newly qualified professionals still require substantial on the job training. Job skills are mastered later, usually under the tutelage of a more experienced practitioner.

If you are studying for an exam which is scored and which will form part of an admission package, consider that the score is only a *part* of the overall package, portions of which (such as grades, performance reviews, etc.) have been already determined over the past few years. Other parts of the package, however, have not yet been determined and remain very much in your control. For example, a winning autobiographical essay and personal interview may greatly influence admission decisions, as will your choice of school. There are so many variables at play! The test score is only a part of the picture. If the other variables are stellar, a marginal score does not knock you out of the running. Conversely, a stellar performance on the exam is no guarantee of admission either, if your other credentials are seriously lacking. The point here is to understand that the exam score is merely one piece of the puzzle, not the biggest and not the smallest piece. Perhaps that notion will dispel some of the pressure associated with taking the test.

Thus, we know that the test is either the last hurdle between you and your professional license, or an integral part of your application package for a graduate program. It deserves your fullest effort in the next few months. But do not attach to it any greater purpose than that. To do so only adds pressure and serves no useful end. Do not treat it, as some are apt to do, as a larger referendum on *anything* — not your professional hopes, dreams or goals.

Understand that professional programs
requiring a scored exam for admission
will also evaluate some or all of the
following five things:

> undergraduate grades
> letters of recommendation from teachers,
>> colleagues and employers
> work experience
> autobiographical essays and personal statements
> special attributes, interests or skills

# 2

# Focusing on the Goal: Preparing to Prepare

*"Commit yourself to your calendared subgoals and preparation plateaus."*

One of the most crucial steps in successfully preparing for the rigors of exam study and the mighty concentration that will be demanded of you is to clearly define the goal and subgoals behind your efforts. Clearly, your *goal* is to master the exam in order to gain your license or enhance your chances of getting into graduate school. As later pages will discuss, your preparation approach may differ depending on whether you must simply pass the exam, or if you are competing for the highest score possible. But the *goal* remains the same, to succeed on that test! Take a moment to express in your own words the goal of your exam preparation. Doing so will help you stay as focused as possible.

The subgoals are shaped as you delve into your studies. They are the smaller, supporting commitments such as how much time each day you will try to allocate to your studies, how far you will get in reviewing your test materials in the next hour, etc. Subgoals also have to do with your commitment to yourself to keep up with the preparation reading or to regularly and punctually attend a preparation course. Subgoals are the composite commitments that help you realize your ultimate goal.

You have a finite amount of time before the actual date of the exam. It may be a matter of weeks or a certain number of months. If you are studying for a legal bar exam, for example, intensive prep courses begin two months prior to the exam date, and are predicated on rigorous daily schedules with an occasional day off for good behavior. Graduate admission exam prep courses (for the LSAT, OCAT, etc.) are structured in a variety of ways and the student can pick the one that suits best: an intensive three week "every other night" schedule, or a weekly class meeting over a period of eight to ten weeks, supplemented in all cases by daily outside study. Independent study can start earlier or later than the commercial course schedules, although starting too early (as in months and months before) or too late (as in days before) makes no sense for obvious reasons — neither approach will yield best results for you.

To the extent you can, start to jot down the goal and subgoals associated with your exam preparation, and then physically plot the subgoals relating to your time commitments on a blank calendar. This way, you will start to visualize the time frame. Your performance during the preparation period will lay the groundwork for your success on the exam, so get a good feeling for how many days or weeks you actually have before you.

If you are reading this book some time before embarking upon your preparation studies (a terrific idea), take advantage of the head start by investigating the schedules and study materials for your exam preparation courses and/or the handbooks and other materials you may use to prepare. Pinpoint the time that you will start your studies. Fill in the calendar based on what you find out.

Once the study calendar is filled in, start to add some personal details. Write down any ongoing commitments or special events that will come up during the period, in order to see what your time frame will involve apart from your study efforts. If you are handling a full or part time job during the preparation period, or are still attending school while preparing for an admission test to a graduate curriculum, add to the calendar any special obligations those commitments will impose. You will quickly understand the priorities competing for your study time.

Unrelated to work responsibilities, you may have continuing or special commitments to family and friends. List any commitment that is a potential time taker. For example, list obligations to attend or (heaven forbid) help plan an event, celebrate a family occasion, or care for a family member. Do not forget to calendar your personal dates as well, such as any standing appointments or time consuming errands.

Visualization of your time frame is helpful for a number of reasons. First of all, it is a healthy look at how you spend some of your time. It shows what emerges as important and what did not make the list. Second and more importantly for you, it presents the opportunity to be proactive about your time, to manipulate the calendar in your favor. To the extent possible, determine what, if anything, can be deferred. Can a project at work or school be postponed to a time after the exam? Can responsibilities for a family event be transferred to someone else? Then again, the value in looking at the time involved as a whole unit lies in your being able to plan for what ever you know about in advance. The general idea is to avoid surprises during the study period, and minimize commitments outside your basic responsibilities. You can make up for any inconvenience caused to loved ones, friends and coworkers after you pass the exam.

As a general rule, you should try your best during the study period to minimize change, too. Now is not the time to start a new diet regime, exercise program or interpersonal relationship (new acquaintances, if they are that special, will respect your short term priorities). Now is also not the time to *end* a diet regime, exercise program or interpersonal relationship. Simply stated, put any major life changes on hold during the study period. This is a time to exert your best, most focused effort and to invest in yourself. Changes are sources of stress, and you will experience enough stress as you prepare for and take your professional exam.

Start thinking about your support network during this preparation period. Will it be a spouse, a good friend, a parent? This is the person on whom you can count for encouragement and support for your efforts, the person who will appreciate your hard work toward your goal and not weigh you down with additional responsibilities or emotional burdens. If you care to, choose a person to keep apprised of your study progress, and report to him or her regularly. It will help you to focus on your efforts.

Do not despair, however, if you feel no one in your immediate world can take on that role and that therefore you are at some sort of a disadvantage. The fact that you are preparing for a professional examination means that you have already accomplished a great deal. Your strength comes from within. Summon that same resolve to push and encourage yourself over this next hurdle of test taking.

By the same token, be selective about the people with whom you will spend your time during the preparation period. So many of us continue to deal with people who have a certain knack to upset us, or make us doubt ourselves, or cause all manner of internal malignancies, that its almost a matter of self-preservation that we should censor out these individuals during times of peak stress and concentration. Let them know that you will be less available, or if possible, totally unavailable during the study period. Of course, one must bow to the realities of modern day living. If the bothersome person can not be selectively removed from your world, even temporarily, due to work place obligations (such as when the person is — of all things — your *boss),* or family ties prevent such relegation, you can only do what you can do.

Look back at the calendar you have filled in. Acknowledge the priority you are going to give your studies.

When you become aware of additional requirements and subgoals imposed by your test prep course or handbook, you should break out the calendar again and pencil them in. Also be sure to note on the calendar where you want to be with respect to certain review materials, and by what date. For example, divide your study materials into sections and note the order in which you will attack them. If you do enroll in a test preparation course, be sure to ask for a syllabus of instruction; it will provide a valuable resource for personal pacing. Be realistic in the calendaring of these preparation "plateaus" because there is no sense discouraging yourself by falling short of them. On the other hand, preparation plateaus are serious business and you should work your hardest to achieve them throughout the preparation time frame.

The calendar is a flexible tool. Many students, new to the world of professional test preparation, find it helpful to spend a week studying first, then projecting progress and establishing subgoals. If the test preparation is a ten week period, for example, give your full effort for one week and *then* fill in the calendar with preparation plateaus. Similarly, if after the first week you can see that the calendar is too optimistic of an expression of your likely efforts over the next few months, realistically revise it.

Commit yourself to your calendared subgoals and preparation plateaus.

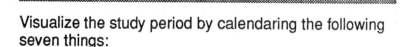

Visualize the study period by calendaring the following seven things:

    time between now and the exam
    exam prep course schedule
    daily exam prep study time
    ongoing commitments
    special events
    standing appointments
    time consuming errands

In your own words, list your exam goal here:

_____

_____

_____

In your own words, list at least eight subgoals here:

1. _____
2. _____
3. _____
4. _____
5. _____
6. _____
7. _____
8. _____

Use the following three calendars to visualize your exam preparation time frame:

*Monthly Calendar*

| Sunday | Monday | Tuesday | Wednesday | Thursday | Friday | Saturday |
|--------|--------|---------|-----------|----------|--------|----------|
|        |        |         |           |          |        |          |
|        |        |         |           |          |        |          |
|        |        |         |           |          |        |          |
|        |        |         |           |          |        |          |
|        |        |         |           |          |        |          |

*Notes:*

## Monthly Calendar

| Sunday | Monday | Tuesday | Wednesday | Thursday | Friday | Saturday |
|--------|--------|---------|-----------|----------|--------|----------|
|        |        |         |           |          |        |          |
|        |        |         |           |          |        |          |
|        |        |         |           |          |        |          |
|        |        |         |           |          |        |          |
|        |        |         |           |          |        |          |

*Notes:*

## Monthly Calendar

| Sunday | Monday | Tuesday | Wednesday | Thursday | Friday | Saturday |
|--------|--------|---------|-----------|----------|--------|----------|
|        |        |         |           |          |        |          |
|        |        |         |           |          |        |          |
|        |        |         |           |          |        |          |
|        |        |         |           |          |        |          |
|        |        |         |           |          |        |          |

*Notes:*

# 3

# Choosing Study Aids, Courses and Books

*"Many students, when preparing for professional and graduate school entrance exams, feel compelled to review in great depth materials used and studied in school courses they have completed on subjects covered by the exam. For the most part, this effort is misdirected."*

You can not do this alone. Even if you could, why would you want to? If for no other reason, you should use study aids to mark your mastery of the tested subjects, and thereby let yourself know where you stand with respect to the material. There are a variety of ways to prepare yourself for a professional exam, and you should review all of the alternatives before picking one or a combination of a few.

But do avail yourself to the expertise of others who have been at this test taking business a lot longer than you. Sure, we have all heard the story of the brainy loner, who read just one instruction booklet from the official testing service and then aced the exam. Similarly, there are legendary stories about brilliant students who do not prepare in the least for these exams and score perfectly. Along with you, I hate these people — if they even exist.

The fact remains that the best study aids help to consolidate your body of knowledge into useful components, give suggestions on approach to exam questions and most importantly, familiarize you with the nature of the test and its questions.

That last point about familiarization is truly the most important. Your score on a professional examination will reflect in large part how familiar you are with the nature of the test and its questions. If you are already acquainted with how reading comprehension, for example, is tested on the GMAT, or how your knowledge of physics is examined on the MCAT, you can devote your efforts during the actual exam to the business of demonstrating that knowledge, instead of spending a portion of your precious time trying to figure out the test maker's *vehicle* for measuring such knowledge. Another advantage of being familiar with the test is that on examination day, you will need to spend very little time on the examination's printed directions; a quick confirming glance that, indeed, the directions you have read before in all those practice tests are the same ones governing the game now, and off you can go, getting right to the meat of the matter faster. For timed tests, this amounts to an enviable advantage.

Evidenced by your reading this book, you consider your test preparation important. Operating from this premise, let's review what study aids are available to you to maximize your test preparation. First, there are a variety of nationally known preparation courses. They are generally offered for all of the "big" exams, including college entrance exams, graduate school entrance exams, real estate licensure tests, state bars, CPA certification exams, and civil service tests, to name a few.

Depending on the exam you are taking, there may be more than one test prep company operating in the area, allowing you to compare their services, methods, costs and reported results. Ask those who have taken a particular course if they thought it was worth it. If the person you ask did well on the exam, ask to what extent the course played a role in that success. You may be surprised by what you are told. Typically, the successful test taker will identify the value of the course in terms of how it organized the student's preparation and how it familiarized the student with the test taking format. Rarer is the response that the student learned volumes of new material relating to the underlying profession. As a matter of fact, in most review courses, the particular body of knowledge tested is presumed to have been taught and learned before. The course emphasis is on organizing that data for quick consumption and short term memorization.

Try to obtain a sampling of the course materials, if the company will allow it, or attend an introductory course or informational meeting. You want to make sure that the operation is organized enough and sufficiently concerned about the success of its students before you entrust it with your precious preparation time. Check also on things like the accessibility of the instructors. Do they make time for students outside of class in order to clarify points and confer on study strategies?

Also inquire about the instructors' credentials to teach the course. Its important that the teacher have some relevant experience with the test, and perhaps some professional experience in the career field associated with the test. That way, class instruction is much more interesting and informative. In the case of graduate school admission exams, test prep instructors are valuable resource people for questions you may have about graduate school applications and interviews or about what it is really like in the field itself today.

If there are study facilities available at the prep center, check on the hours and ask when the most crowded times are. What arrangements do they make to accommodate students during such peak times? Ask, too, if there is any type of financial aid available or special payment programs for those putting themselves through school. There is no question that these courses can be expensive. If the reputation of the test prep company is solid enough, consider becoming a student representative, responsible for signing up your peers. Typically, representatives get a break in course pricing. Similarly, if the courses are conducted by video or audio instruction in remote locations, there may be some tuition adjustment available to a student who acts as the session "facilitator," taking roll and playing the tapes at the appointed time.

Know the advantage and, at the same time, the disadvantage of enrolling in one of these courses — it imposes structure on your studies. Some students welcome such structure with open arms because they may feel overwhelmed trying to prepare a coherent study schedule on their own. On the other hand, structure means being at a certain place at a certain time, doing the assigned homework (and feeling guilty for not having done it) and so on.

For a test taker who is fully employed while preparing for the exam, the guilt factor can be considerable. After a long day of work, having to once again show effort and energy for an evening or weekend course is tough. Then again, better to have the material spoon fed to you by the instructor, absorbing what you can, than kidding your tired self that you will accomplish as much, if not more, working alone.

If you are in the market for a prep handbook, they abound. They run the gamut from thirty pound monsters written by the large publishing houses to flimsy pamphlets marketed by former or current experts in the field. Also included in this category are "books on disk" and other computer programs which offer exam preparation. If you are going to prepare for your exam by the exclusive use of one of these books or programs, evaluate it in terms of two key components: explanation of approach and practice tests. The rest of the material may be useful for other purposes (by, for example, listing graduate schools in the country and average test scores of admitted students), but will not directly contribute to your success on the exam itself.

Explanation of approach is defined as tips and strategies for solving the test questions — everything from how to diagram, outline or deduce an answer, to how certain tested sections are weighted against others. Weighting information will assist you in devising effective study strategies, because there is no sense spending a great deal of study time getting frustrated on lesser tested areas. Good explanations of how to approach an answer are the key to understanding why you got an answer wrong and will also help you save time in figuring the answer to questions you can otherwise get right.

While evaluating a prep book, read a sample question and the explanation for the answer. If the explanation is written clearly and logically, if the author has done a fair job of showing you why or how the answer is what it is, the book will serve you well. In the case of computer reviews, try to talk to someone familiar with the program, or get some sort of guarantee before purchase, because these programs vary in quality and are difficult to evaluate before loading them on your computer.

The second component is the volume of practice tests in the book or computer program. Although the importance of taking numerous practice tests is covered elsewhere, its importance can not be overemphasized. The study resource you choose must have a sufficient number of practice tests to allow you to gauge your progress and get a feel for exam conditions (developing a sensitivity for time restraints, long term concentration requirements and performance fatigue). In addition, the act of taking the test and later correcting it helps solidify your knowledge of the material being tested. Depending on the exam for which you are preparing, practice tests will follow each section or chapter of exam material covered and should also appear at the end of the book, as a full length simulated exam. It is important that the test prep book or computer program contain several of these full length tests, as the last thing you want is to run out of preparation material before the exam itself. On the other hand, it makes no sense to buy several test prep books just to stock pile different practice exams. Having so many tests and then, due to time constraints, not being able to get to them all, breeds anxiety. Rather, figure on making additional test prep purchases later, if you find you need the extra tests.

Many students, when preparing for professional and graduate school entrance exams, feel compelled to review in great depth materials used and studied in school courses they have completed on subjects covered by the exam. For the most part, this effort is misdirected. Although relevant to the subjects on the exam, this course work is often neither coherent nor "bare boned" enough to make your review of it efficient. For the MCAT, for example, your course work may have included the physical properties of certain elements on the chemistry chart, but a good review course or handbook will streamline the information and present it more effectively. Similarly, reviewing volumes of old accounting notes in preparation for the CPA exam is not as efficient as studying an updated outline prepared by the test taking prep pros. The reason is simple: your professional exam will not — can not — go into the same depth on any subject matter studied in a classroom. There simply isn't time on exam day! Instead, it seeks to measure *breadth of knowledge*, a slightly different concept requiring different preparation materials.

Remember that in choosing study aids for your test preparation, you are making an investment in yourself and in your success on the exam. With careful consideration and advanced inquiry, you will find the study aids that will prove most useful to you.

To check out a commercial test prep course, do the following eight things:

ask about course instruction methods
ask about results achieved by former students
get costs and schedules for the courses
ask former students about the course's effectiveness
attend an introductory class, if possible
check on the instructors' credentials to teach
ask about on site study facilities and crowded times
check on financial aid and discount tuition

To decide if a test prep handbook or computer program is worth it, check that it includes the following four things:

basic explanation of the exam and how it will look
tips and strategies for solving the test questions
clearly explained exam answers
full length practice tests with answer key

# 4

# Maximizing Study Time and Study Efficiency

*"The whole challenge to studying effectively is to make the study time as active as possible."*

Once you have made the commitment to study earnestly for your exam, you owe it to yourself to be as productive as possible during your study sessions. The truth is, you already know the circumstances under which you study best, and for each person they are slightly different. If the only place you can absorb the material is with your shoes off, on the couch, with the din of a TV game show in the background, so be it. If, on the other hand, you need a quiet, library type surrounding to best absorb material, you probably know that about yourself, too.

You have already achieved a great deal, evidenced by your pending plan to take a professional exam, so go with what you already know works. To give you some additional tips, this chapter is full of suggestions and innovative ideas on how to maximize your study time. Try as many suggestions as you can, and find those that yield the best results.

First off, choose the study environment that suits you best. It may be the quiet of the library, the comfort of your home, your workplace after everyone else has left, at a friend's workplace, in an empty college classroom or at a test prep course center which offers study facilities. It must be a place that holds a minimum of distractions, or it will not serve you well. To some, being at home is too close to the phone, the fridge, the television and neighbors. To others, home is an ideal study place because you can do a load of laundry or take care of a small chore in between review sessions and practice tests. Also at home, there is no commute to the study place and you can be as comfortable as you like. Of course, these comforts cut both ways, in that they may make you feel too relaxed or distracted. Clearly, you must have discipline to study at home, and you alone know if you have it.

The advantages of doing your studies at some of the other places mentioned are that they require a special effort on your part to be able to study there at all; by requiring you to transport your books, papers and other materials, these places may help you focus on the task at hand. Statistical surveys indicate that the study environment plays a significant role in stimulating short term memory retention, and short term memory retention is largely the name of the game. Take seriously your choice of where you will study.

Interestingly, many students find that slightly changing their study environment stimulates productivity. For example, if you do choose to study at a library or study center, occasionally change your seat. If possible, change to a different library or study room. You will be surprised by the way your mind may associate concepts you study with the different location, enhancing memory retention.

It does not matter where you settle in to study as long as you are diligent and give it your best effort. But how can you give something your best effort, especially studying, when tired? Therein lies the second most important component to successful study — you *must* be alert when you hunker down with the books. Good intentions do not count here. If you fall asleep in your notebook or spend your time fighting off heavy eyelids, your study time is a waste. In that case, you are probably better off with a quick cat nap of approximately twenty-five minutes followed by a renewed effort with the books. Any longer of a nap is too great a snooze. You will feel more groggy when you wake up than you did before you drifted off.

Of course, in a perfect world, everyone would have eight to ten hours of peaceful sleep each night and such stress free days that any time devoted to studying could not help but be productive. Right. We all know that one of the casualties of modern living is the average number of hours we get to sleep each night. The amount continues to decrease over time, as our responsibilities increase and the total number of hours in a day to meet those responsibilities does not. If possible, make a good night's rest a priority.

Be judicious with your time in the later evening, and do not squander it on unproductive things like watching television for the sake of watching it, or accepting social engagements that will keep you out later than you know is best. If a social commitment poses the risk of a late night, invite the help of other attendees to see to it that you are home by a certain hour, or maintain your independence from nocturnal friends by bringing your own car or taxi fare with you to the event. That way, you can always cut out when you should.

But let's say you have done all of that, and in spite of your best efforts, your body wants to shut down every time you set up your studies. What can you do? Get creative. If your most productive time, even when tired, is in the morning, get up a little earlier and apply that prime time to your exam review. If you are still in school, you may have the luxury to rearrange your classes or your extracurricular activities to save your most productive waking hours for the books. Do not even *try* to study after eating heavily. Take an invigorating walk to digest first. Remember that a warm study environment can make you drowsy, so open a window or take off your sweater. If you are a coffee, tea or cola drinker, learn how to harness to your advantage the effects of caffeine. Some people can bank on the slight rush they get from a good cup of java, and those folks are wise to schedule study sessions shortly after having one. We have already discussed how a short nap might help. Generally, any quick physical activity that gets your heart rate up (moving your arms in a circle for a few minutes, running in place, stretching different body parts, etc.) will boost your study staying power. Above all, motivate yourself with a reminder of how important your successful performance on the test is.

Settling in to study, do all you can to facilitate your focus on your review materials. Minimize potential interruptions by advising others you are unavailable. If at home, turn on your telephone answering machine and turn down the volume. If appropriate, put a do not disturb sign on your door. Some students, to cut down on outside noise, use ear plugs. It may seem like an extreme measure to take, but you would be amazed at how it enhances your ability to hear yourself think!

Ear plugs are available at most drug stores, and, courtesy of modern science, they are inexpensive, sanitary and convenient. It is important to remove from your desk any extraneous items, including your briefcase or book bag, and any other unrelated materials. At best, they get in the way; at worst, they make tempting distractions. You need to spread out on a clean surface, one that is not cramped or cluttered. Choose an upright chair that is comfortable but not too cushy. Lastly, make sure your lighting is adequate.

The whole challenge to studying effectively is to make the study time as active as possible. Taking a practice test, for example, is a very active way to study because it requires you to analyze information and do something with it. Reading a chapter of technical information, on the other hand, can be treacherously passive, almost to the point of being a time waster, if you cannot stay focused. You must do what you can to make your studying, whether it be practice test taking or technical reading or something in between, as *active* as possible. There are a few ways to do this, and with practice, these methods will become second nature to you.

First, if you are reading background material, use a highlighter pen to underscore the important parts. The act of highlighting will make your reading more active, and will also streamline a later review of the material. After highlighting, outline what you read. The outline can be very brief, even if no more than marginal notes. Again, the act of writing will confer greater memory retention. While you read, try to summarize mentally what you have just read, and ask yourself questions about the material as you go along. Working with the material in this way may marginally slow your progress, but it is a time saver in the long run because it cuts down the number of times you will have to review the same material.

If the material lends itself to the use of flash cards, make sure you have some on hand whenever you study. Make a card on key concepts, questions and definitions you come across. Just writing the card will help you retain the information, and the cards then make handy review tools for standing in supermarket lines, waiting for appointments, and quick glances before bed. If a concept is particularly difficult for you, discuss it with another person. Preferably, that person will have experience in the area you are studying, or is currently studying the same things you are, but seems to have a better grip on the particular subject matter. If no one familiar with the material is available, discuss it with an outsider. Sometimes, just hearing yourself go over the concepts out loud facilitates your thought processes and the ideas may become more clear.

Know your study time tolerances. If they are reasonable, do not force yourself to exceed them. Depending on the schedule you develop and the nature of your professional exam, you will allocate a certain number of hours each day to your study prep. If you know that after three hours of hard work your brain turns to gelatin, then there is no sense regularly pushing yourself beyond that. Organize the material you want to cover in segments, such as certain designated chapters followed by a set of practice questions followed by preparation of a brief outline, etc. You will enjoy a feeling of accomplishment as you finish each segment. If you do not finish all the work you set out to do during the period allocated, ask yourself if you are aiming too high (and adjust your segment timetables) or if you are lagging behind due to some impediment (like tiredness, interruptions, etc.). To the extent possible, minimize or remove the impediment!

Make the distinction between needing a break and reaching burnout for the day. Many times, a short break will refresh you and recharge your ability to concentrate. Bring a favorite magazine or book with you when you study, and if you successfully complete a segment, reward yourself with a five or ten minute pleasure read. Accomplish a short task that is quickly and easily done, such as writing a birthday card or thank you note, preparing a "to do" list or cleaning out your backpack, purse or briefcase. Take a brief walk or chomp on a favorite fruit. Sketch, draw or doodle if you can. If you are in the library, roam the isles for a few minutes and find an interesting book to browse. Rewards, if properly fit in with study segments, can prolong your study sessions. Just be careful that they do not eclipse the real purpose for which you are there. Do not let them exceed ten to fifteen percent of your intended study time, and for heaven sakes, do not feel obligated to take them if you are "on a roll."

On the other hand, if long hours of concentration come naturally to you, then your only challenge will be how to organize your studies to cover the material effectively — long hours alone will not do it. You must be sure, as previously discussed, that your study time is as active as possible. Tackle the most demanding materials first, leaving the less complicated or less demanding stuff for later. Review the material you have recently studied to keep it fresh in your mind, either by rereading previously highlighted sections of your materials or scanning the outlines you have been preparing. If you are taking a prep course, frequently review the syllabus and be sure you are keeping up with the suggested workload. By doing so, you will maximize what you gain from the course, and it will be a source of reassurance to you that you have covered the material in the order prescribed by the pros. If you are using a test prep book, photocopy off the table of contents and keep a running tab of your progress on the materials by writing in the margin the date you finish reviewing each part.

Effective use of your study time is one of the most important components to success on the exam itself. Some days will feel more productive to you than others. That is just the nature of things when you put in hard effort over an extended period of time. But over the long haul, your steady, earnest efforts will pay off.

Six suggestions on where to study:
> library
> at home
> your workplace after everyone has left
> at a friend's workplace
> in an empty college classroom
> prep course study facility

Six ways to fight tiredness when you study:
> take a cat nap
> rearrange your schedule to study when most awake
> avoid studying in a warm or stuffy place
> take a brisk walk before studying or in the middle
> have a cup of coffee, tea or cola
> do a few minutes of quick, physical exertion

Six things to do to help focus yourself on your studies:
>  minimize potential interruptions
>  try using ear plugs
>  remove distracting items from your study area
>  do not study in a cramped or cluttered place
>  choose a comfortable chair
>  use adequate lighting

Six ways to study more effectively:
>  use a highlighter pen to underscore important parts
>  briefly outline what you read
>  mentally summarize as you read
>  use flash cards for key concepts and definitions
>  discuss difficult concepts with others
>  know your study time tolerances

Six things to do to take a quick break from your studies:
>  glance at a favorite book or magazine
>  accomplish a short, easy task
>  take a brief walk
>  eat a piece of fruit
>  roam the library isles for a good book to browse
>  sketch, draw or doodle

# 5

# Anatomy of a Multiple Choice Question

*"First, recognize the inherent advantage of having the four or five alternative answer choices right in front of you — the correct answer is already on the page, and all you have to do is find it!"*

When you think about it, multiple choice questions are a pretty ridiculous way to measure a test taker's competency in a professional field. After all, can the grader ever really be sure that a student's correct answer represents the culmination of thorough analysis, rather than just a damn good guess? And what about a multiple choice question's relevance to the real world? Does an ailing patient ever ask a doctor to diagnose his condition by choosing one disease from among four lettered possibilities? Of course not! A multiple choice question is most often used for convenience in correcting an exam, not because it is such a superior testing tool.

But be that as it may, we still have to live and work with this particular test taking format, as a battery of multiple choice questions is by far the most popular way to examine large test taking groups. Fortunately, there are some hidden advantages to the format, as well as some handy universal rules of thumb to remember and employ when you take a multiple choice test. Use them to enhance your performance on the exam.

First, recognize the inherent advantage of having the four or five alternative answer choices right there in front of you — the correct answer is already on the page, and all you have to do is find it! Knowing the answer is contained in the question is a great relief compared to being asked to supply an answer on your own. With the given alternatives, you readily know how the answer should be expressed (unless how to express the answer is what the question is all about, as in a question testing definitions, or asking for the best summary of a main idea).

You also get, by way of the answer choices, what amounts to four or five helpful memory joggers. This advantage is helpful in case your reading of the question leaves you pretty cold. By glancing at the answer choices offered *before* you tackle the question, you reap another advantage of this format — you can then read the question with a focused eye as to what component parts are going to be important to the answer and what amounts to less important "filler." Also, there are no essays to outline and write, or back-up calculations to make. The only thing a multiple choice test grader looks at is whether you got the right answer, no matter how you got there. Given all these pluses, its no wonder that some students breathe a big sigh of relief when they see this format!

Knowing that multiple choice questions make up all or a share of your exam, keep the following tips in mind to enhance your score.

First off, remember that age old notion about sticking with your first guess. On a multiple choice test, it's usually right. Only change an answer you have already chosen if the original answer was no more than a wild guess *or* if you find that you originally *misread* the question *or*, if the question required a numerical calculation, and you discover that, upon second look, you did not calculate correctly. Studies show that in other than those three instances, the first hunch was more often right than it was wrong.

To prove this postulate to yourself, take a fair number of practice questions, and then, *without correcting your answers*, take the exact same set of questions again. Although you will get a little bored, you will also come across some answers that, upon second look, you would like to change. Mark those questions and only change the answer if your reason for doing so falls within one of our three acceptable reasons (wild guess, a misread or a miscalculation). Now correct the whole test. Observe your ratio of right versus wrong answers for the questions *on which you had doubt*. Your first hunches will probably prove right a majority of the time.

The second tip is to remember that each question's answer is independent of your answer for a previous question, meaning that you should not fret just because you have not chosen a certain lettered response in a long time. Believe it or not, students do get uptight about this lack of symmetry on their answer sheets, because they cling to the notion that probability dictates that over the long haul, lettered alternative "a" should appear as many times as the lettered alternative "d," and so on. And that premise would be true if the act of creating a test question, and the placement of four alternative answers, were perfectly random acts. But they are not. Test makers subscribe to all different notions of how to construct a good test, and that may or may not involve their attention to answer placement. One thing is certain, the test maker did not stay up late to calculate an even distribution of lettered answers. Do not worry about looking for that on your answer sheet. Treat each question as an independent variable, and do not be influenced by the frequency or dearth of any particular lettered answer. If you do, you will dissuade yourself from choosing the correct answer in favor of some under represented letter pick, especially on a question that is a really close call. In addition to that, you will make yourself nuts by the time you finish the test!

We have already touched upon the third multiple choice test taking tip: glance at the answer choices for a quick moment before reading the actual question. This approach orients your mind quickly as to the nature of the question and will influence what you emphasize when you read the question itself. This tip does not take a lot of time, if executed properly, because you are not laboring over the answer choices up front. You merely glance at them. You will be rewarded by the use of this technique in almost every type of multiple choice question, including ones that ask for calculated answers.

For example, if the answer choices all deal with summarizing a main idea, you would read the question with an eye toward summation. If the answers all deal with your choosing an outcome or result, read the question with that analysis in mind. When you see numerical responses for answer choices, circle or mark relevant numbers given in the question, so you can readily refer back to them in constructing the calculation you need for the answer. By reading the answer choices in advance, this technique will save you precious seconds, which over time add up.

The next tip is a subset of the prior one: if the multiple choice question itself is lengthy, start to mark key points with your pencil as you read, so you can readily refer back if needed. By taking that advanced look at the answer choices, you will get a preliminary feel as to what is important in the question and what probably is not. As a general rule, dates should be marked, and so should proper nouns. If "buzz-words" of your professional field are used in the question, mark these, too, as they are often key concepts you will want to refer back to when analyzing the question. If a chain of events described in the question can be quickly reduced to some sort of shorthand in the margin, that is a valuable mark to make too. After practice with quick marks, you will find that they come easily to you. This technique will considerably streamline the time you take to refer back to the question.

Tip number four is to draw a line through any answer that is clearly wrong. That way, you will not reread that answer choice along with the remaining contenders, saving a bit of time. You will usually be able to quickly rule out at least two contenders, leaving your eye and brain to focus on the remaining choices. Make sure you read the answer pick a second time, as you are lining it out, to make certain you have not *misread* it. If you have read it correctly, trust your gut feeling that the answer is wrong and do not waste valuable time second guessing yourself that maybe it is right after all. Choose your answer among the remaining alternatives. This system stresses the "first hunch" theory and will save you time.

The next tip is to get used to bubbling in answers on a long answer sheet with a number two lead pencil, because that is the answer format on most standardized exams. Many students, in taking practice tests, will mark their answer choice on the test question itself. On exam day, that answer pick must then be transcribed to the answer key, in the correct place, quickly and efficiently. The act of bubbling in an answer does take extra time, even if its seconds per question, so it makes sense to have some experience with it. If you do a sloppy job of bubbling, the test may be misinterpreted by a most unsympathetic computer, or have to be hand corrected by an aggravated human being. Avoid those possibilities. Be neat and precise with your answers.

The last helpful hint is one of the most important. Keep careful track of your time and do not spend an inordinant amount of it on any one question. Rather, pick your best guess and move on. When you arrive at a real challenging question, whatever you do, do not leave the answer space blank. Instead, remember to enter an answer, while your pencil and mind are stopped at the question, in order to avoid any misnumbering of answer choices down the road, and to cover yourself with at least a guess. That way, you have a shot of getting credit, even if you can not return to the question later. Similarly, take advantage of those times when you nail the question and its answer right on the head with relatively little time. Those questions are a gift from the exam fairy, and you should not squander your good fortune by lamenting over the question or thinking there must be more to it than that. There isn't, so move on.

To develop the required multiple choice question pace with your practice tests, start by establishing what the re-quired pace is. Simply take the time allotted to you to complete an exam section, and divide it by the number of multiple choice questions in the section. Most standardized exams will require that you operate at a clip of one question every two minutes, give or take. Of course, that allocation is an average; some questions are answered right away, and the net time savings are applied to the more challenging questions. Take a few practice tests to see where you land on the time scale. If you run short of time, push slightly harder but try to prevent a corresponding slide in reading comprehension. Practice perfects pace here, because multiple choice test taking is a learned skill. If it helps, reset your watch to the nearest full hour when you begin the test, and mark every thirty questions with the time by which you should reach that question. For example, if you have two minutes per question and you begin your practice test at eleven o'clock, you should be on the thirtieth question by noon, the sixtieth question by one o'clock, etc. If it becomes clear to you that you are falling short of time as you reach these markers, speed up to the extent you can.

Let's say that in spite of mammoth speed training, you fall short of time on the actual exam. Do not panic, lest it affect your performance on those questions you *are* tackling. The last tip to remember is to bubble in an answer for every question, whether or not you get to it. Most standardized professional exams do not carry a penalty for a wrong guess. Accordingly, by bubbling in at least something, you have a one in four or one in five shot of getting credit, with no down side. That's better than no shot at all. If you have a brief moment to skim the answer choices (but not concentrate on the question), chose the answer that employs a familiar concept or strikes you as an answer that, standing on its own, seems to make reasonable sense. If you are down to the last moments of the test, with test proctors breathing heavily over you as they try to collect your answer sheet, then bubble in answers at random. Obviously, picking answers without reading the question and down right random bubbling are the least desirable ways to arrive at an answer choice, but in these desperate times, having given any answer is better than having given no answer at all. Before employing this suggestion, however, confirm that there is no *penalty* for a wrong answer. If there is, you are better off leaving the question unanswered unless you have had at least a brief opportunity to analyze it.

Use of these tips, coupled with your systematic review of the underlying concepts being tested, should greatly enhance your performance on the exam.

When the test format is multiple choice, the test taker has the following three advantages:

the correct answer is already somewhere on the page
answer choices can work as memory joggers
in giving the answer, you do not have to show your
analysis or calculations

Seven tips for enhancing your score on multiple choice tests:

stick with your first answer unless your reason
for changing it is one of the reasons discussed
in this chapter
remember that each answer is independent of previous
answers
glance at each answer choice before reading the
question
mark key points of lengthy questions, as you read it
draw a line through any answer that is clearly wrong
practice bubbling in answers on an answer key
keep careful track of time remaining on the test

# 6

# Anatomy of an Essay Question

*"Hone your timing skills on essay exam questions, because spending too much time on one and leaving others to whither can be deadly."*

Essay exams have been known to strike terror in the hearts of test takers, due to the remote chance that, after carefully reading the question, the student may find he or she has absolutely nothing to say on the subject! On the flip side, an essay exam can be a joy when you really know your stuff, because the test format is a terrific vehicle for showing the world how much you know, and how good you are at succinctly discussing all that you know. This chapter dissects the essay question and offers a standard approach for answering one. It also offers tips and suggestions to ward off panic if you come up against an essay question that has you stumped.

The typical essay question on a professional exam is a presentation of facts and figures, calling for the student to spot and decide issues brought up by the fact scenario. Usually, there is no clear cut, short answer, and the student must compare and contrast theories, or analyze a conflict and reach a conclusion. In addition to worrying about the content of the answer itself, the student has to worry about presentation, grammar, punctuation, handwriting, timing, and other variables.

To fully understand how to write a winning essay answer, it is useful to understand how essay answers are graded. Like a mine sweeper, an essay test grader will quickly review your essay answer, looking for certain main points that are already listed on a "model answer" outline. That is why, if an essay question suggests that you discuss three different aspects of a problem, your time is more profitably spent hitting all three areas, compared to doing the most complete, bang up job on two and failing to mention the third area all together. Your order of presentation is not nearly as important as the grader's ability to find the point somewhere in the essay. Only then can the grader give you credit for recognizing that point and analyzing it. The grader sweeps over your essay, looking for these points, and then rapidly goes on to the next exam to be graded. Your job, while answering the question, is to hit as many relevant points as possible and to make grading the essay for the reader as easy as possible.

The trick to making an essay response easy to grade is organization. It really is critical. In many cases, organized mediocrity will score higher than disorganized brilliance! The reason for this phenomenon is that in grading essay exams, there is a subjective element known as the human factor. Unlike a machine grading a multiple choice test, the human mine sweeper/grader gets tired (and as a consequence may miss points which are not made clearly) and the human mine sweeper/grader gets frustrated (when points are made but lack logical cohesion with the rest of the essay). As a result, organized mediocrity often wins out. Of course, *you* will achieve nothing short of organized brilliance on your essay response, but isn't it nice to know there is a safety net?

An organized essay answer fits into a standard answer "shell." You can rely on this shell to lend organization to your essay answer and to keep you on track. No matter what the subject, the shell is comprised of these main components: an introduction, an issue statement, an analysis of relevant concepts, an application of the relevant rule or rules, and the conclusion. This shell is adaptable to just about any essay question, no matter what the subject matter. By writing your essay response with these component parts in mind, you will stay organized and garner maximum scores. By availing yourself to this shell, you will also have a leg up in countering the panic that grips students when they realize that they have no idea how to answer an essay question they have just read.

To illustrate, suppose you are taking a state bar exam, and you are asked to analyze the probable outcome of a fact scenario in which two parties are suing each other over a problem debt. You are asked which party will prevail and why. Interestingly, choosing the "correct" party in this instance does little to advance your credit point total on the question, because the meat of the matter is contained in your *analysis*, not which party you choose. If you named the correct winning party and then went on to the next question, you would get little credit. Compare that to a multiple choice question, where even a correct *guess* is handsomely rewarded!

As explained, the treasure trove of points lay in the analysis, which you should start by an introductory statement as to what the outcome should be. Next, identify the issue suggested by the fact scenario. If there are several, indicate that this issue is the first of four that you will address. For example, if the question is testing your knowledge of certain legal principles, you might write "the central issue here is whether the corporate shareholders can be held liable for the corporation's debts." Next, cite the applicable rule of law which governs the situation, such as "generally, corporate shareholders will not be held personally responsible for the debts of the corporation." If there are exceptions to the general rule which bear on the matter at hand, discuss them as well, as in, "however, there are certain exceptions to the foregoing rule which may bear on the outcome of this case." Now, discuss the rule and the exceptions, if any, as they apply to the facts in the essay question. Finish the essay answer with a short concluding statement.

If the question requires that you discuss several points suggested by the facts, simply reapply the answer shell to each point analyzed. You will find that this shell is helpful on just about any professional exam that asks you to analyze a conflict or discuss the ramifications of a certain fact pattern. Try it with practice questions, under strict time limits, and you will find that it serves you well.

Hone your timing skills on essay exam questions, because spending too much time on one and leaving others to whither can be deadly. The best way to allocate time is to divide the number of essay questions by the amount of time given, and further divide that amount of time as follows: spend 15% of the time allotted for that question on outlining the answer; spend 75% of the time on writing the answer; and spend the last 10% of your time rereading and proofing your work. In a typical exam, in which you must answer three questions in three hours, that translates into approximately 10 minutes to outline an answer, 45 minutes to write up the masterpiece, and about 5 minutes to check your work. If the question requires you to discuss subparts, adjust the formula so that you spend quality time on each subpart. Of course, a one hour question with four subparts is more like a short answer session than an essay response, since allocating your writing portion among four areas will leave approximately 11 minutes per subpart!

Lastly, remember that above all else, you are writing to please. Keep the handwriting neat. Use correct grammar. Use periods and paragraphs liberally, so the reader does not get lost. Now is not the time to pontificate or alienate. Now is the time to write a damn good essay, one that is well organized, sincere and easy to score.

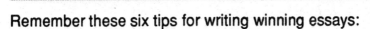

Remember these six tips for writing winning essays:
> organization is the key to a high score
> outline before you write
> keep careful track of time
> write neatly
> use correct grammar
> discuss as many points as are suggested by the question

# 7

# The Fine Art of Making and Saving Time

*"Your best ally during the preparation period is organization. The more organized you are in your study approach and in your life in general, the more you will find that you can get done in the time you have."*

This is the hard part. If modern life would only give you enough time to sit and concentrate on the books, you could score in the stratosphere! The problem is that you have tons of competing priorities, and fitting in the studies will take a lot of doing. Worse, as is often the case, you are not sure that the people around you will cooperate with your study efforts or indirectly undermine them by adding a few more problems or responsibilities to the heap you already handle.

If you subscribe to the premise that those students who do well on professional exams are those who have had sufficient opportunity to study and to put their minds to the material, you will agree that there is great value in effectively organizing your life before the exam so that you, too, will have that time to study. If you make the effort to clear away chunks of time in your day to devote to your studies, you will be richly rewarded by your efforts.

There are two secrets to making time to study, and they are probably already intuitively known to you. The first secret is that productive study must be your new priority, period. It should fit on your personal list as high up as it possibly can go, nestled somewhere *below* food, shelter and clothing, but definitely *above* social life, leisure time, and delegable chores. The second secret to making time to study is to examine and rearrange current time allocations and commitments to accommodate this new priority. In other words, you must be willing to make certain physical adjustments in your daily and weekly schedules which in turn enable you to reclaim wasted or inefficiently spent time, or time spent on things that are now less important. These adjustments include but are not limited to reassigning tasks in order to open up pockets of time, redefining tasks to make them less burdensome or less time consuming to you, and re-evaluating the relative importance of certain tasks, in light of your new study priorities.

Let's examine first how you implement your new study priority. So many professional exam candidates, when faced with the daunting task of exam prep, ask themselves how in the world they will fit *that chore* into what is already a busy life. Yet your power to fit it in is enormous.

To illustrate, suppose you woke up one morning feeling lousy. You might then make it a priority to see a doctor. If, after examining you, the doctor informed you that you needed surgery, you would probably find a way to squeeze that in, too, even though we both know how busy you are. If the doctor told you that your condition was life threatening, and surgery was required immediately, you would fit it in *that day*, wouldn't you? Its all a matter of priorities. You would do whatever was necessary to make time to have life saving surgery, including rearranging your schedule, cancelling your competing obligations and delegating others. If you chose to discuss the situation with family and friends, they would likely offer encouragement and ask if they might help you with your other responsibilities, too. Right?

Now, I am not suggesting that you lie to your family, friends and coworkers by telling them you are having life saving surgery and will be unavailable for the next few months, when all the while you are perfectly fit and just want to be left alone to study! I am merely suggesting that your commitment to properly prepare for your exam begins with your treating preparation as a priority, and fitting it in as high as possible on your list. The surgery example is meant to show that even the busiest among us have the power to accommodate new priorities.

You must be aggressive and jealous of your time. That is how you implement your new study priority. Be judicious about saying yes to anyone or anything that is a potential "time taker," and be firm and self-assured about saying no. You will find people will respect you for your commitment to your new priority. Inform people who might be interested or have the power to temporarily lessen your load that you are under the gun studying for a professional exam. If appropriate, invite their assistance in making more study time available to you. You will be surprised by the response you get from those who feel they are making a contribution to your success by taking responsibility for something you would otherwise do. And you should always do a good job of acknowledging that contribution, so they might offer help again before the exam is over! Make sure you tell them the date of your exam, so they can appreciate the finite nature of your challenge.

Recall the calendar you filled out in Chapter One. Look specifically at the activities, commitments and obligations you have during your preparation period. To the extent possible, pare this list down to its most minimum. Ask other family members for help with obligations that also benefit them. Ask to postpone until after the exam anything specially required of you at work or school, that you know can sit a while without too much detriment. Find ways to rearrange your schedule to create pockets of one or two straight hours that you can commandeer for study time.

Can you go overboard on the time reallocation? Possibly, since you can not spend every waking moment studying and preparing. If you tried to do that, you would get bored and burnt out in short order. In fact, fulfilling small responsibilities to yourself and others during your study period can be a welcome distraction and give you a feeling of immediate accomplishment or gratification. After spending time on a seemingly unending task like "studying," it will feel great to mark off from your list some concrete chore.

Prioritizing is a learned skill. To prioritize effectively, you must first get a handle on everything that you need and want to accomplish in a day. Write a list of those items, and put a box around the things on the list that are not negotiable by *time* or by *nature*. For example, on a typical Thursday, your 8:00 am to 6:30 pm workday is not negotiable by time or by nature, since you must put in the full day, and your duties at the office can not be curtailed to allow you any study time. (Perhaps your lunch hour has a little wiggle room, but using it for study purposes is a matter of personal preference; some people need their lunch hour to clear their heads, while others have the uncanny ability to wolf down a sandwich and spend the balance of their time with review materials.) Similarly, if you are currently enrolled in school, daily class attendance will probably be nonnegotiable by time and by nature. However, also on that typical Thursday, you may have to run two errands, prepare dinner, call your aunt and spend "quality time" with your spouse or kids. With respect to your studies, you also want to read two chapters of your review materials that evening.

Look at each item you have written on your priority list, and ask yourself if any is negotiable — meaning *changeable* — by time or by nature. For example, is the second of your two errands something that you could do later in the week, by combining it with another errand you know you will have? Or perhaps a friend or family member could accomplish that particular errand for you. That would be a negotiation *by nature*, because upon re-examination, you are changing the nature of the priority. If the dinner preparation could be simplified, or the telephone conversation with your aunt could be made briefer, that would be a negotiation *by time*, because in those cases, you are not changing the nature of what you will accomplish, you are simply trying to find a way to accomplish it in less time. By negotiating by time or by nature, as circumstances permit, you can begin to assert your new priority. You should find pockets of time opening up.

Once the time and nature negotiations are finished, you must next *order* the items on your list. Order them in such a way that will reflect their relative importance, one against the other, while all the while deferring to the time block in which each should be accomplished. Thus, you are ordering your listed entries in light of the "bigger picture" of how they rank against each other and the applicable time constraints. For example, you need to prepare dinner in order to serve it within a certain time period, and you must make that call to your aunt before it gets too late. These are time considerations, and they will dictate, to a certain extent, how you order your list. Other factors influencing the order of your list may include degree of personal interest in the task, geographical location, degree of importance, etc.

To continue the previous example, you know that your first errand can be accomplished on your way to errand number two, or vice versa. Or perhaps errand number one is absolutely critical, but errand number two can wait for now. Accordingly, errand number two is put at the end of the list, and there is a chance that you will not get to it that day. As you can see, these considerations will variously impact your list.

In light of all these factors, prioritize. When you are finished, your list will become a logical road map for you to follow. It will reflect your priorities and prompt you to accomplish them in an effective order.

All the prioritizing in the world will not help if you simply have too much to do. If that is the case, you must delegate some of your responsibilities, if at all possible. To delegate a responsibility to another is to remove yourself from the details of getting it accomplished, while still retaining an interest in it finally being accomplished. Overachievers, interestingly, are poor delegators. To them, to delegate is tantamount to some sort of admission that they could not handle the burden. But in reality, it is nothing of the sort. It is simply a wise allocation of resources to recruit or assign someone else to accomplish something for you, in order that you may accomplish something else — like studying. You may find an opportunity to delegate a few responsibilities at home, such as marketing chores or cooking duties. Similarly, you may be in a position to delegate at the workplace, especially if you already have a professional position, supervising a staff of workers. The whole trick here is to delegate one or two time consuming items, which in turn serve to free you to pursue something else, such as hitting the books.

Your best ally during the preparation period is organization. The more organized you are in your study approach and in your life in general, the more you will find that you can get done in the time you have. Better still, one of the dividends of organization is that you will find you have more time in your day than you thought you did.

There are no special tricks to being better organized. It is all a matter of keeping proper track of time, responsibilities and things, in an attempt to control matters instead of having them control you. Your efforts to stay organized must be constant and sincere. Keep a calendar and reminder list in close reach. Make priority lists, and revise them as circumstances warrant. Some students review and revise their priority lists on a daily basis, using them to get acclimated to the day ahead and to remind themselves of what they hope to and should accomplish that day. You should make priority lists often and stick to them.

Another tip to staying organized is to make decisions on how to best structure your day before someone else comes along and does it for you. For example, if you do not have a clear sense of mission about what you are going to accomplish one Saturday afternoon, you are a sitting target for someone — whether it be a family member, friend or coworker —

to come along and exert some sort of pressure on you to accommodate *them* during that "unclaimed" time. This intrusion will take away any power you had over those hours. By contrast, had you already organized your day, you would have stood a much better chance of assuming control over the intrusion, and at a minimum, worked it in where it fit best in your day, and not upon someone else's demand.

Another tip to staying organized is to commit yourself to structure — in your studies, and, at least for the time being, in your personal life. Structure anchors you and reassures you that you are doing the right thing at the right time. It deters unwelcome distractions. For example, you may choose to structure your exam review so that you work through a certain number of chapters of test material each day before you go do something else. With respect to your personal life, you might choose to structure your daily schedule so that you go to bed at the same time each evening and rise at the same appointed time each morning. That way, your body chemistry has to do the least amount of day to day physical adjusting while you demand more and more of yourself. By abiding by this structure, you can more accurately plan for what you can accomplish each day.

If you are meeting family obligations while still working or schooling *and* preparing for a professional exam, you are carrying the fullest load. There are some special tips for saving time with family obligations that you may want to consider.

First of all, do not be afraid to negotiate and delegate some of the responsibilities you do have. Perhaps a cleaning chore can be streamlined or delegated. Have a pow wow with your spouse (and kids, if they are old enough; and parents, if they depend on you for assistance during the day) and enlist support for what you are doing. You can enlist this support in two ways. The first way is to familiarize your family with the nature of the exam. Although *you* may be up to your gills in professional terms and specially learned concepts, your family members only know about the test what you have told them. So make a point to discuss the exam, the types of questions you will have to answer, the volumes of material you are expected to know, and the amount of time you have to prepare for it. Even show them one of the practice exams. In other words, *quantify* your challenge.

The next thing to do in order to garner your family's support for your efforts is to ask family members if they have any suggestions to help you carve out more time in your day or week to devote to studying. You may be surprised by the help they offer you. It may be anything from a simple promise to keep things calm during your study hours (by occupying the kids, screening phone calls, etc.), to a pledge to do that week's marketing for you. If their helpfulness advances your goal, you should graciously accept it. And do not spend time worrying if the chore gets done in a way slightly different than you would have done it. That would be swapping a time taking activity for a time taking worry, with no net gain to you. The point here is that family members can be a great resource in meeting your exam preparation challenges, and you can use their good faith energies to lessen your load.

Surveys show that households expend a significant amount of time and effort on the daily preparation, eating and cleaning up of dinner. Unless you live alone and subsist on a diet of fast foods, or you participate in a college campus "meal plan," you will recognize this time taker right away. It may be profitable, then, to review a few time saving techniques for use in the kitchen. For starters, do not forget about the value of a good list — when you shop, plan meals, assign clean up chores, or just about for any other organizing purpose. A shopping list with grocery needs for at least three full dinners and one back up dinner plan is the best rule of thumb.

Planning three full dinners sounds fair enough, but what is a back up dinner plan? That's soup and sandwich night; or a macaroni and cheese from a box night; or a pasta with a commercially prepared pasta sauce night. These are the dinner menus you keep around to avoid those last minute, waste of time, just one or two item trips to the market. Some of those menus have a longer shelf life than you and me combined, so you know you can count on them in a pinch! By staying well stocked in these items, you are keeping your market trips to an efficient minimum.

There are several tricks to saving time in the preparation of meals. If you can productively use the time around the house for some other purpose (like studying or cleaning or tending to a chore), then emphasize recipes that take less than five minutes to prepare, but take long, *preferably untended*, cooking time. To illustrate this concept in the extreme, look at TV dinners. "Remove foil," and you have finished preparing. The cooking time is long, and untended. But you can make wonderful dishes that involve a little more of your creativity but not a lot of time. For example, bake a chicken. Simply wash it, pat dry, season with salt, pepper, garlic, thyme, or any other seasoning that strikes your fancy, and bake at 375 degrees for approximately one hour. Want to get really fancy? Add baked potatoes or cut up some carrots, celery and onion in the baking pan. With a minimum of preparation, you have a great meal. To save time later, make large portions and freeze them. Then on days when you are really running short on time, you defrost, warm and serve. There are now many commercially prepared sauces to which you add beef, pork or chicken and bake for about an hour. Because the spices and other ingredients are already in the sauce, the preparation time is less than two minutes! A microwave is a big time saver, and there are good recipes available for casseroles, steamed vegetables, and meat dishes. Microwave popcorn can be a quick, in between meals snack that is fast to prepare and, if chosen with care, nutritious, too. Want to really cut your cooking time down? Buy a crock pot. You can load it up in the morning with anything from chicken to beans, from soup ingredients to mouth watering chili. Then it cooks on the low setting all day, piping hot when you arrive home for the evening.

If, alternatively, you need quickly prepared menus, keep your wok near. You can cut up a variety of foods found in your refrigerator or freezer, be they frozen, raw or already cooked, and bring them to spicy life in a good wok. Keep a few Asian sauces on hand and you can prepare a great meal in under twenty minutes. Spaghetti can be prepared quickly if need be, as can thin fillets of fish. Do not overlook the speed with which you can prepare a good omelette, stuffed with all sorts of extras you find in the house. (If cholesterol worries you, just make the omelette from egg whites or commercially available egg substitutes.) If weather permits, barbecuing is a quick way to prepare a hot meal, and clean up is minimal. Thus, given some thought, dinner preparation times can be drastically reduced without great compromise in taste or nutrition. By careful planning, you may save considerable time with dinner.

In general, you will find that you get better and better at making and saving time as you practice the tips in organization and prioritizing discussed in this chapter. These are learned skills, and you should make the effort to take control of your study preparation time by acquiring them.

To effectively implement your new study priority, do the following five things:

> be aggressive and jealous with respect to your time
> pare down to the extent possible your list of
>    commitments unrelated to your studies
> learn to negotiate priorities by time and by nature
> get organized and be proactive in planning your day
> prioritize, prioritize, prioritize

To get and stay organized, do the following six things:

> keep careful track of time, responsibilities and things
> keep a calendar and reminder list
> make priority lists and revise them as needed
> review your priority list each morning
> decide in advance how to structure each day to your
>    fullest advantage
> commit yourself to structure

To save time with family responsibilities, try the following three things:

> negotiate and delegate family chores and
>    responsibilities
> enlist support for your goals from family members by
>    quantifying your challenge
> keep lists for marketing and other errands

To save time with dinner preparation, try the following six ideas:

> choose quick to prepare menus
> make extra portions and freeze them for another meal
> use a microwave
> try using a crock pot
> make stir fry meals in a wok
> barbecue if weather permits

# 8

# During the Long Haul: How to be Your Own Best Motivator

*"Know up front that flying high and feeling low, sometimes on the same day, are natural parts of any long term, sustained effort like studying for a professional exam. The trick is to not only expect this rocky road, but to plan for it."*

Studying is an admittedly long and arduous process, and it is not particularly interesting or immediately gratifying. So how are you expected to maintain a functioning level of confidence and enthusiasm for this stuff, over the course of one, two or even three months? It is not easy, on top of everything else, but you have got to become your own best motivator. *You* have to be the one that pushes yourself just a little bit further, the one who helps yourself through the difficult times and the one who rewards yourself for the successes.

73

For those who already have a solid support network comprised of family and friends, this element of self motivation is still important. For those students who do not readily have that kind of support, it is critical. To elevate your sense of mission and zeal in connection with your exam prep, consider the following techniques and strategies. They will help you better perform throughout the preparation period and on test day itself.

The first step in maintaining your motivation is to commit yourself to the preparation process. You must firmly believe that your academic and career aspirations are worthy of your time and effort in preparation for this exam, and that the time you do spend preparing is a worthwhile investment in yourself. There is nothing more debilitating and poisonous to one's motivation than a quick flash of self-doubt about your ultimate performance on the exam. That thought quickly unleashes a motivational free fall in connection with the task at hand. After all, if you do not think you will do well on the exam, why waste an evening (or a day or a week) studying?

The point here is that you have to believe enough in yourself and your abilities to give yourself permission to work hard. And then stick to that conviction. Only then will you be able to feel confidence in the decisions you make to structure your day to make time for the studies. Only then will you have the self-assurance to inform others that you are less available than usual, or simply unavailable for a certain amount of time. If you believe the goal to be worthwhile, you will act on that belief. Given the way professional exams are structured, there is no question that you will benefit on exam day from your dedication of time and effort in preparing. Do not lose sight of your goal to do well on the exam, and do not doubt that you deserve to — and you will — achieve that goal.

The next tip in maintaining your motivation is to expect the ups and downs of the studying process. Know up front that flying high and feeling low, sometimes on the same day, are natural parts of any long term, sustained effort like studying for a professional exam. The trick is to not only expect this rocky road, but to plan for it. Be ready for those days when you are just not in the mood for studying, when the mere thought of opening up your review materials will make you break out in hives. If you have been making steady progress over the course of the past few days, and you need to take a break from things, go ahead! Do something that really gets your mind off the test, and do not feel guilty about it, either. The mind, like the body, needs time once in a while to recuperate from its workouts. As long as you do not abuse this philosophy, a break can be beneficial.

Because ups and downs are a normal part of the intensity of the preparation period, be equally prepared for the up turns. Those are the times when you are really on a roll, when things make sense, and you are mastering the material. In that case, don't stop! Maximize the momentum by lengthening your scheduled study time, or rearrange your review materials to tackle even more challenging stuff during the same study session.

Another tip to staying motivated is to maximize your number of "fresh starts." Studies show that the average adult attention span peaks and wanes in cycles of approximately ninety minutes. This is not to say that studying more than one and a half hours at a time is unproductive, it merely suggests that breaking a three hour study session into two sessions of one and a half hours each may lift your concentration levels, attitude, and generally increase the aggregate productivity of your efforts. Try a few study sessions designed to maximize your fresh starts and compare your energy levels with those during extended study. See if you experience any advantage. To some, a fresh start is the most invigorating way to bring new life to the study effort. Of course, excessive fresh starts will get you no where. All that means is that you are not giving yourself the opportunity to become engrossed in your studies before you close the books for another break. Be sensible as you structure your study sessions, including how you will maximize the fresh start advantage.

Stay motivated by setting and meeting realistic study goals. As you prepare for the exam, allocate what you need to accomplish over the amount of time you have for the preparation effort. Do everything possible to meet these preparation subgoals, adjusting your allocations as circumstances warrant. Make the subgoals concrete. Rather than a subgoal to "study for two hours," write down "finish review of chapter ten and take fifty multiple choice practice test questions." By being precise with yourself, you will concentrate on accomplishing the task at hand, not just watching the clock. Remember that for this system to work, your study subgoals must be realistic, not too light and not too heavy, because meeting some easy subgoal or falling short of meeting subgoals that were impossible anyway does nothing to motivate and spur you on. Meeting *realistic* subgoals does.

Keep the exam and the whole study thing in perspective. Nothing can sap your motivation quicker than the lather you can work up about the pending professional exam — how you have to do well, how unprepared you are, how depressing it is to study day in and day out and feel guilty if you don't, how no one is suffering as much as you are, etc. By the time you are done, you will have wasted valuable mental effort and have nothing to show for it. There is no question that you are challenging yourself in order to better yourself, and that is a worthy goal deserving of all your might. But whether you take this exam or not, your life and life in general will go on. Who knows what options you will pursue in the future? You may take the exam again, or reevaluate your chosen professional path altogether. One thing is clear — this exam is not the beginning, the middle, or the end of the world.

How simple it is to remind you of that, and how impertinent of me to do so, since this book is about dedicating yourself to preparing and successfully taking your test! But sometimes a whisper of reality helps you keep things in perspective, and along with everything else in this pressured time, you must do that. Take a moment and count your blessings and think about what is really important to you and how much you have already accomplished in this world to even be in a position to sit for the exam. Do not wait for some unfortunate thing to occur to remind you how fortunate you already are; your appreciation of that now will refresh and motivate you in your studies.

Do not let others distract you from your goal or bring you down. "Distractors" come in two forms. Physical distractors physically waste your time and keep you from accomplishing what you need to. Mental distractors inadvertently or even purposefully say or do something designed to preoccupy you while you worry about, feel guilty because of, analyze, and just plain work through whatever it is that they said or did. Both types of distractors wreak havoc on your studies, because your study productivity plummets when you are mentally preoccupied with something else. The time is just plain wasted.

The difficult part of dealing with these distractors is that they come and go, and are at times the very people from whom you would expect support for your efforts. For example, your best friend may tell you something disturbing and the next day take up a valuable hour of your time discussing it with you. Similarly, your spouse could choose the most inopportune moment to complain that you have not had the chance to spend enough time together. There is no automatic malice on the part of these distractors, which makes dealing with them even more difficult. You must draw strength from the known worth of your commitment to your goal —and by extension, subgoals — and pick and chose to what degree you will allow these folks to get in your way. Considering the circumstances in that manner, you have a lot more power over the situation, since *you* are going to decide if the distraction should be tolerated or indulged, or just plain ignored.

Of course, you will bring to this calculation all of the factors you innately know, such as the relative importance in your life of the person distracting you, and the relative merit of the distraction. But at least you will have the luxury of deciding where the distraction will fit in your priority scale. If its low enough, it should be discarded without hesitation, because your other commitments are too important. It is said that no one can make you feel guilty without your permission. By extension, no one can mentally distract you without your permission either, and in most instances, you should withhold that permission while you study and dedicate yourself to your goal. In the least, do your best to defer these distractions until after the exam, especially when the exam is coming close. Be blunt at these times and inform the person that you are choosing to worry about their problem on the date after the exam. Invite them to check back then. You will be surprised by the response you get, because few people are proactive like that in dealing with distractors.

To stay motivated, design an effort/reward system. This is a modern innovation on the carrot and the stick routine, which basically calls for you to determine in advance what small incentive would motivate you to keep studying and stay productive. If you satisfy yourself in this regard, by meeting your review goal, or giving the studies that extra hour, or accomplishing whatever else it was that you decided to do, then reward yourself. By way of reward, you might choose any number of things that give you simple pleasure, such as watching a favorite television show (that perhaps you taped with your video cassette recorder, so you can watch it at your convenience, without commercials); taking a short walk through the park; purchasing a favorite magazine; or enjoying two scoops of your favorite ice cream. Be as creative as you can, and enjoy the reward.

When you do choose a reward, for heaven sakes, choose sensibly! An ice cream reward that is enjoyed for the moment but only means big time guilt later is *not* an appropriate reward. Neither is a reward that requires you to spend a significant amount of money, unless of course you have it. Keep in mind that rewards are meant to be little celebrations of your hard work along the way, so do not take advantage of this notion by, for example, planning a whole day off just because you outlined an extra chapter the day before. That would effectively negate the previous day's progress.

The last and most potent technique for staying motivated during the long haul is to accentuate the positive — about yourself, your personal circumstances and your efforts relating to the exam. Think positively and optimistically, even if its tough to do at first. Be your own best friend and learn to encourage yourself. Mentally concentrate for a few moments on the best image of yourself that you can, and project that image. Along those lines, try remembering, and — for a moment — reliving, some successful experience, and think for a moment how the same factors that contributed toward that past success can and will help you now. Then apply yourself to your studies with a renewed sense of confidence. After all, you are in the process of becoming even more accomplished and successful!

Staying motivated throughout the study and preparation period takes hard work, but your efforts will pay off in more productive study sessions and better overall exam performance.

Concentrate on the following nine things to help yourself stay motivated during the preparation period:

    commit yourself to the preparation process
    self-censor doubt and emphasize self confidence
    expect the ups and downs of the studying process and
        plan for them
    maximize your number of fresh starts
    set realistic study goals and meet them
    keep the exam in perspective
    do not let others distract you from your goal or bring
        you down
    design an effort/reward system for yourself
    learn to accentuate the positive

# 9

# The Power of Familiarity: Practice Test Taking

*"Practice test taking gets you down into the trenches with the test makers, affording you the opportunity to hone your test taking strategy."*

Sheer knowledge of the material being tested is not enough to score well on a standardized professional exam. To do well, you must know *how* the material will be tested. Once familiar with the testing vehicle, you have a tremendous advantage! First of all, no time is wasted on trying to understand the test directions. If you have taken practice tests that are accurately patterned off the actual exam, you will know the test format right away. Secondly, anxiety levels on exam day stay low because you are already familiar with the whole test taking routine. You will know what is expected on the exam, and you will have a pretty good feel for how long you have to complete each part.

The most effective way to familiarize yourself with the exam is to take practice tests. Under exam-like conditions. *Lots of them.*

There are some obvious advantages to taking practice tests. First of all, they force you to interact with the material. From that interaction, you get a pretty good indication of how well you can work with the tested concepts. Secondly, they give you a feel for the time pressures involved. On an essay test for example, practice gives you experience in analyzing a question, outlining an answer and coherently presenting the answer within the allotted time frame. With multiple choice questions, practice gives you a feel for how quickly you must work through each question and select an answer from the four or five given alternatives.

There are some not so obvious advantages to taking practice tests, too. The most important one is that practice tests are an incredibly effective self-teaching tool. You will remember getting an answer wrong if you take an additional moment to understand why and how another answer is correct. If you see the same or similar question again, you will get it right — particularly if you believe it is some sort of "trick" question, one whose answer is predicated on some nuance that you would not have appreciated but for seeing it before. If your professional exam asks for essay responses, practice tests offer a huge hidden advantage. Having prepared practice answers in the past, you will be comfortable with the essay framework and the form the answer should take, no matter what the subject being tested. Not only that, but you will have a good notion what constitutes a winning answer, and perhaps just as importantly, what does not.

Practice test taking gets you down into the trenches with the test makers, affording you the opportunity to hone your test taking strategy. You must make practice tests an integral part of your preparation routine.

Now that we have established that the practice tests are valuable, how should they be worked into your preparation? Tossing your review materials in favor of daily practice tests will probably not do the trick. You first have to spend time reviewing the basics of what is being tested. But if you think you have spent quality effort on the review materials, then dig out a practice test dealing with that subject. If you have limited time to take the whole test, pro-rate the time and test questions in order to get a feel for the required pace. For example, if there are one hundred questions in a three hour time limit, work through one-fourth of the questions in one-fourth of the total allowed time. If you finish with time to spare, check your work carefully. If you run out of time, self-assess the problem. Are you reading too slowly or taking too long to diagram or to calculate in the margin?

Most students, when asked, can readily identify their particular test taking weakness. On subsequent tests, concentrate on yours. See if you can read a little faster or diagram a little quicker, or even pick up your handwriting speed on the essay responses. Those saved seconds translate into minutes over the entire exam, and those minutes can be valuable in allowing you to get to the last few questions or to check over your work.

Practice test taking is fatiguing, too. After giving it your concentrated effort for a fair block of time, your mind inevitably wanders from the test, and your focus wanes. This result is justified, when you consider that test taking is not the most entertaining thing to do. But on professional exams, especially those lasting longer than one three hour session, stamina is everything! If on test day you are a star performer in the morning but succumb to fatigue in the late afternoon, your score will be lower than what it would otherwise be, if you were allowed to take the exam in a series of fresh starts.

Fatigue is the test taker's most insidious enemy. Push yourself during practice tests to overcome the fatigue and recognize when it starts to impact your performance. Combat the fatigue factor just as you would any other physical limitation. Start out slowly and build up your stamina level. Fortunately, your adrenaline flow on the day of the exam will do a lot for you in this regard — you will be amazed how much farther you can push yourself when you know it really counts. But putting that benefit aside, learn your own way to pump yourself up so your performance on the latter parts of the exam are as solid as your performance at the start. If your concentration wanes, take a moment, close your eyes, and refocus. Open your eyes slowly and stretch out your writing arm. Adjust your seat and inhale deeply to supply your brain with the oxygen it needs. Block out the rest of the world, especially your mental distractions and worries, all of which will wait for you to finish the test. Make up your mind to give the remaining portion of the exam your best shot. Now reread the question you were working on and go to it!

Once you have finished a practice test, get maximum value from how you correct it. If you have taken a multiple choice test, try the multiple choice answer reduction system. Correct your answer sheet against the answer key, marking the ones you got wrong. Do not do anything further with the answer key. Instead, go back to the test itself and *retake* the missed questions. This time, of course, you have an additional clue that the answer you previously chose was wrong. After trying each missed question again, correct that set of answers. Keep retaking missed questions until you get them all right. On a multiple choice exam offering four alternatives, there may be one or more questions that you keep retaking until, by process of elimination, you *must* arrive at the right answer! Now go back to the answer key and study first all the explanations for questions that took the most number of tries to get right. Those questions represent areas on which you still need to concentrate, either on the underlying concepts, or how the concept is tested on the exam. Go over every explanation, even if you got the question right, in order to cover points that you may not have considered in answering that question, and to confirm that you got the answer correct for the right reasons and not due to some fluke.

Correcting a practice essay question is a little trickier, but there is a certain method by which you will gain maximum insight into what constitutes, at least in the test maker's opinion, the optimum answer. Then you can independently evaluate how close you came to the same answer in your own essay. As suggested in a previous chapter, it is a good idea to prepare a quick outline of the points you will cover in answering an essay question. That approach is sound because it keeps you on track and keeps the answer somewhat organized. If you prepared a brief outline of the answer, turn to it when you correct your essay. Now prepare a brief outline of the *model answer*. Compare it to your own and you will quickly see if you have covered the same points. Of course, your order of discussion of these points is not the most important part. What is important is that these points occurred to you when you sat down to answer the question! If they did not, bone up further on the area tested and try another practice test.

The value of practice test taking cannot be over-emphasized. It is a part of any quality preparation effort. To reap their benefit, be sure to incorporate practice test taking sessions in your preparatory studies.

You get the following five advantages from taking practice tests:

> you save time on the actual exam
> you become familiar with the exam and thus
> > reduce potential anxiety
> you learn to adjust to the time pressures
> you gain a great diagnostic studying tool
> you become familiar with winning essay
> > answer frameworks

To maximize the practice test's benefit as a learning tool, try the following six step multiple choice answer reduction system:

> take a practice test of multiple choice questions
> correct your work, marking those that you got wrong
> retake the missed questions
> correct those that you retook
> continue until all questions are correctly answered
> carefully study the answer explanations for the most
> > often missed questions

# 10

# Examination Day Strategies

*"Whoever said that kids can be the cruelest never
met a bunch of adult test takers on exam day."*

It probably does not even need to be marked on your
calendar, because the date of the exam itself is already
indelibly etched on your brain. All your preparation and hard
work, the emotional roller coaster and the anticipation, it all
comes down to the big exam day. In the case of quite a few
professional tests, the big exam lasts *days*. Proper planning
and the proper mind set during this crucial time will
contribute to your overall success.

Let's examine the time frames immediately leading up to
your taking the test. At some point the day before, you must
put away the books and practice tests and end your test
review. This act is unbelievably difficult for the conscientious
student, who wants to gain maximum advantage out of the

time remaining before the exam. Just remember that it is a doubtful premise at best that one can actually learn anything of value — meaning anything of score raising potential — that late in the game. What you *will* raise is your anxiety level, especially if on the night before the exam you do not perform well on a practice test, or if you get confused about any test material you choose to review. There is very little to be gained in the eleventh hour. Why put yourself through that debilitating experience? Instead, feel confident that you have worked hard during the preparation period, you deserve to do well, and you will do well.

If by early evening, or before, you have put away the books, what in the world should you do with all that anxious time? First, schedule in an early bed time, and make up your mind right then that you will enjoy a very sound night's sleep. Plan to settle down for bed at least one hour before you want to actually be sleeping, and make all the arrangements you have to in order to keep this commitment to yourself. If you find you are too uptight to sleep, just lay there and rest your eyes. Concentrate on relaxing each part of your body in logical order, and think positive thoughts about your test day ahead. Set two different alarm clocks to ring at the appropriate time the next morning.

If there are loads of time left before going to bed, rent a lighthearted video or go see a movie. Choose to do something that is enjoyable and relatively mindless. Do not talk about the pending exam with a friend (that's not mindless, its nerve racking) and do not undertake anything stressful or distracting. Some students find a gym workout in the early evening calms them; others prefer an evening of television comedies. Although it can be an enjoyable pastime, reading a good book is not your best relaxation choice, even if it is a page turner.

You will be doing a tremendous amount of reading under pressure the next day, so it makes sense to steer clear of that same activity the night before. Do not let well intentioned family or friends monopolize your time with good luck wishes. Keep your conversations with them short and direct. The longer the conversation, the larger the possibility that they will say something to you that is unintentionally distracting to your confidence and success. Remember, this is *your* exam and will reflect *your* performance. You are entitled to exert maximum control over pre-exam factors.

Eat a good dinner the night before the exam, preferably in the earliest evening. Emphasize complex carbohydrates and protein over the other food groups, because carbohydrates and protein are sources of steady energy. (Long distance runners often "carbo load" the evening before a big race.) For heaven sakes, do not eat anything out of the ordinary. Now is not the time to try some new, spicy dish at your favorite take out joint. And do not even *think* of trying to concoct something new at home. Stay with the tried and true, the familiar. To minimize any possibility of stomach discomfort the night before or during the exam, make sure everything that you do eat is fresh, properly prepared and well cooked. The stomach butterflies are one thing; a bad case of food poisoning, quite another.

Steer clear of caffeine in the evening, so it does not get in the way of your sound sleep. If you are a caffeine drinker and have come to rely on your daily dose, consider tapering off the stimulant in the week before the exam (but not completely stopping, lest you suffer headaches and other withdrawal symptoms). Then, on test morning, you will get double mileage from your morning's fix!

On the morning of the exam, think at least one wonderfully positive thought before you get out of bed. It should revolve around the fact that you are ready for the exam, that you deserve this chance to prove yourself, that you have prepared well, and that *it will go well*. If you can not think of your own related positive thought, tab this page in the book and reread it on exam morning. It is imperative that you develop a sense of confidence about your performance. Follow your normal morning routine, keeping your eye on the clock. Eat a satisfying breakfast, preferably foods with some holding power, like high fiber cereal, hot or cold. Be very judicious about drinking liquids before the exam, because students often find that their kidneys go into overdrive on the big morning. There seems to be some metaphysical connection between anxiety and the urge to pee. Do not exacerbate matters by downing an extra glass of juice.

Take only what you need for the exam, and leave the extraneous stuff at home. Typically, admission tickets of some sort are required, as are a few reliable pens and number 2 pencils. You may want a small pencil sharpener, too, and a clean eraser. Remember to take your driver's license or some other form of positive identification, and also remember to take anything else noted on the test admission ticket itself. You might consider bringing along a portion of that day's newspaper, so you can read something before the exam. The newspaper serves two purposes: it will take the edge off your nerves before the exam, and it will also discourage other students from disturbing you with their intimidating tales of endless hours of exam preparation.

Most professional exams are administered in blocks of three to four hours, with short breaks. If you think you might get hungry sometime during the test, take a candy bar with you, too. It will mask hunger for a while and provide you with some instant sugar energy if your brain starts to wane. In this case, sugar, like caffeine, is another stimulant which can be harnessed for better exam performance. Although a little more cumbersome, a piece of fruit (something quiet and quick, like a banana) will do the same thing. The up tick in your blood sugar will give you some instant energy. But realize that a sugar "high" will be followed later by a sugar "low." Hopefully, that will only come after the exam is over. In the meantime, this quick energy booster will counter hunger or falling stamina.

You should definitely leave your study notes and review materials at home. Curiously, on the morning of the exam, some students become so emotionally attached to their review materials that a good crowbar couldn't separate them. Even if they do not get a chance to look at these papers, they are comforted just knowing they are near. Leave it all home, or back at your hotel room, because you are not going to absorb from them anything worthwhile on the day of the exam. Often, proctors at the exam site will require all books and other extraneous personal materials to be checked in or deposited at the front of the exam room anyway. Those items just become one more thing to worry about. And heaven forbid someone make an accusation that you used them in some way to cheat.

Leave for the exam site in plenty of time. You must allow for a margin of error. If you have a commute to the exam, factor in detours, road delays and parking problems. Allow too for last minute registration or other paper work at the exam site. Some students, to minimize any chance of exam morning commuting delays, stay in a hotel room in close proximity to the exam site. This option is particularly attractive to those taking professional exams more than one day long. Check with the local hotels for special student rates.

Staying in a hotel is an especially popular choice among bar examination candidates, who have to endure two to four days of test taking. On the appointed mornings, they have breakfast in their room and then they take the elevator to the exam! If you do stay in a nearby hotel, request that the staff install a small refrigerator in your room. You can load it up with your morning milk (and/or coffee cream), juice, cereal and fruit, and if the exam schedule includes a lunch break, some luncheon meats, sandwich breads, cheese, lettuce, etc. Coupled with a coffee/hot water maker, you will have everything you need for quick and convenient meals on exam day. You will not have to worry about room service foul ups, and you will save a few dollars, too.

Before you go into the exam room, go to the bathroom. It may help to take the edge off your kidneys. Hopefully, you have a bladder of steel, and you will not be distracted by the need to visit the bathroom during the test. But at least if you do, you will have learned the way there. When you settle into your seat at the exam, get comfortably situated and familiar with the room. Note how many rows you sit away from the rear doors, and where the proctor tables are. These details are important if you do have to go to the bathroom during the exam. By noting carefully where you will have to sign out and where the exit toward the bathroom is, you will more efficiently handle your exit and re-entrance during the exam, saving time and anxiety.

Listen carefully to all the directions, especially any special directions having to do with exam security. To misstep here is to cause unnecessary confusion and anxiety. For example, you may be required to give handwriting samples and finger prints, or told to inscribe ticket numbers on all your exam materials. Some examiners require that you put one form of photo identification on your desk as you take the exam, so it can be checked by a passing proctor. The test takers want to know that it is you taking this exam, and not someone whom you have paid handsomely to suffer for you.

Remember the advantage you will enjoy because you are familiar with the test directions and format. Confirm that what is asked of you is the same thing that has been asked of you in all those practice tests and proceed directly to the questions.

The number one foul up among multiple choice test takers is to get off track and bubble in an answer on the wrong line. The magnitude of this disaster can only be appreciated when you discover it with just minutes left on the exam, or worse, when it goes undetected and yields a horrendously low score. Check every time you enter a multiple choice answer that you are doing so on the correct line. Every time. Repeat the question number as you find the answer number. For example, if you decide the answer to question 28 is "b," mentally say "28-b" as you enter it on the answer sheet. Do this mental exercise *every time*.

The number two foul up on any professional exam is to misallocate your time. You must wear a reliable watch and you must, at a minimum, note the time you start and the ending time for the particular test section. Scribble it down somewhere, unobtrusively, and make sure your progress is steady. After several practice tests, the required cadence will become second nature to you. Nevertheless, keep an eye on your time. The great temptation on the essay portions of these professional tests is to spend too much time on one essay, to the detriment of the ones that follow. Remember, there is no prize for the "perfect" essay answer. Rather, consistency is always the big winner. If you exceed your time allocation on one answer, wrap it up quickly with your conclusion or leave an outline of your remaining points. You will undoubtably receive some additional partial credit. Then get to the next question.

The number three foul up is succumbing to panic. That inevitable knot in your stomach that grows into passing heat flashes followed by massive doses of self-doubt, culminating in serious amnesia. It typically hits at the beginning of the exam, before you have gained your momentum. It may be brought on by one or a series of questions that you simply have no idea how to answer. First, realize that panic is a close cousin of adrenaline, and just like adrenaline, panic can be harnessed. If the first portion of the exam calls for an essay response, panic may ensue if you think you have nothing to say. You must overcome the panic if you are to give the exam your best shot, and overcoming the panic is the ultimate in mind over matter. For an essay test, concentrate on aspects of the answer you *do* know, no matter how remote they seem, and start to write them down. If a multiple choice question has stumped you, pick an answer, no matter how fuzzy or incomplete your understanding of the question — lest you commit the number two foul up, discussed above — and then move on. Tag this question in some way and return to it if time permits.

In dealing with panic, you must reassure yourself with the following two truths. The first truth is that you and all the other test takers are in the same boat. If you have not studied a certain concept being tested, or are having trouble answering all the questions within the time allotted, chances are that the rest of the room is too. And professional tests are almost always scaled to the performance of the entire test taking group, so failing one or more sections does not necessarily mean failing the exam. If enough students miss the boat on a tested section, it is more often than not thrown out from the final scoring. The second truth is that you know more than you think you do. Take a deep breathe, calm down, and relate the question to a body of knowledge that you *do* know. If you are at a loss on an essay exam, discuss that other information, and how it relates to the question. If you are struggling with a multiple choice question, evaluate which answer looks reasonable in light of what you have studied.

And now a final word about interacting with peers on exam day. Whoever said that kids can be the cruelest never met a bunch of adult test takers on exam day. To boost their own levels of confidence, they say and do things to each other that are utterly contemptible. There is the standard intimidator, who thrives on intimidating others with his claims of superior preparation or experience with the exam. There is the standard distractor, the student who will suggest in some pseudo-caring way that you do not look as well as you should — that your eyes are looking bloodshot or that you look pale — all in an attempt to disrupt your concentration as you think about such baseless and distracting comments.

How dare these people be allowed to operate in the close confines of the testing site! Yet they do, and you must be ready for them. Identifying the behavior is half the battle. The other half of the battle is to avoid it completely. If someone begins to discuss the exam with you, simply look that person straight in the eye and say that you make it a practice not to discuss the exam on test day. Or just be rude by excusing yourself and walking away. Do not make yourself an

95

available target by sitting or standing alone and doing nothing with yourself until exam time. Read the newspaper you brought with you, or browse a magazine. Hang out with a trustworthy friend, or spend the time writing yourself a note about how well you plan to do on the exam. Stay occupied and aware, and do not fall prey to these wrongdoers.

By keeping these exam day tips in mind, you will be amazed at how well the day goes for you!

The night before the exam, do the following six things:

by early evening, put away the books
schedule in an early bed time
set two different alarm clocks to ring the next morning
eat a hearty dinner
plan a relaxing evening
steer clear of caffeine

The morning of the exam, do the following six things:

think a positive thought before you get out of bed
eat a satisfying breakfast
be judicious about drinking liquids
take only what you need to the exam
leave for the exam site in plenty of time
before settling in for the exam, go to the bathroom

While taking the exam, be careful not to fall prey to the following three biggest test taking foul ups:

on multiple choice sections, getting off track and
bubbling in an answer on the wrong line
misallocating your time
succumbing to panic

# 11

# Post Exam:
# The Mailman Cometh

*"One of the toughest aspects of waiting for results
is what to do if circumstances require you to make
any decisions before you get them."*

Just when you think it is safe, after the rigors of exam preparation and then finally taking the test and being done with it,
a slow but gathering storm starts to collect in your mind —
how did it really go on exam day? Did you do as well as you
needed to do to achieve your goals? Are you worthy of
achieving that goal? And on and on and on. It can really take
a person down, because these distracting doubts will come at
a time when the test is over, but before you have received any
results. By this point, how you did on the exam is no longer
in your control. But it may be weeks, even months before you
learn your fate. How do you deal with this special torture?

For starters, no post mortem. In Latin, this phrase literally
means "after the death." Today, it refers to the practice of

rehashing the exam after it is over, and trying to figure out how well you did. *The exam is over*, so it will serve no useful purpose to analyze aspects of it after the fact, *especially* with fellow test takers. It will only make you frustrated and angry if someone discusses some aspect of the test that you do not recall or, worse, some aspect of the test that you very well do recall — and what you recall about it was the way you interpreted the question or answer differently! Meanwhile, your friend the test expert will sound incredibly astute about whatever the subject is, and you will wallow in doubt and disappointment for having blown it on the exam. *For heaven sakes, do not discuss test questions or answers with anyone after the thing is over*. It will take strength and discipline not to join in these types of discussions, but it is well worth the effort to protect your sanity. A critical time to exercise caution in this regard is immediately after the exam, when everybody spills out all their pent up exam anxieties discussing specific questions and answers. To get caught up in that can only do harm, not good.

Instead, practice a little positive thinking. Take great pride in the fact that you were qualified to take the exam, and that you did indeed take it. In many ways, the triumph is in the attempt. It reflects your determination to stick to it and do what it takes to succeed. Mentally decide that you did as well as you could do on the test, and that you deserve a good result. Because you do not yet have any feedback on your performance, you should think as optimistically as possible. Evidencing a belief in yourself, as long as you are not arrogant, is contagious. When others ask how the test went (and they will), tell them that you gave it your best shot and cite the date by when you expect the results. No one is entitled to know any more about the exam than that, unless you want to tell them. By giving the date you expect your results, you are politely deferring any further discussions.

One of the toughest aspects of waiting for results is what to do if circumstances require you to make any decisions before you get them. For example, many students take graduate admissions exams around the same time that they are choosing the graduate schools to which they will apply. Knowing your test score would be an obvious advantage here, since it would influence where you might apply. Similarly, if you are lining up job interviews after taking a professional qualifying exam, you would benefit greatly by knowing how the exam went. The best advice is to defer what you can, hope for the best and plan for the worst. In the case of choosing graduate schools, check admission deadlines to see if there is still time to apply to additional schools after the exam result is available. That way, if your exam performance, once known, is out of sync with your school choices, you still have time to make adjustments on the school list. As a general rule, your graduate school choices should include at least two back up choices (schools you think you can pretty easily get into, based on your existing credentials and an adequate test score), three realistic school choices (schools you have a competitive shot of getting into), and two dream school choices (schools you would love to get into if you could). With this formula, your bases are covered.

Decisions regarding job interviews should be handled the same way, only forget the advice to defer what you can. In this case, take advantage of the unknown and shoot for the skies. If all your other credentials are in good order, and you project confidence and optimism, your interviewer will assume the best with respect to the exam result. You may even generate a job offer before the result is known. This would give you great leverage to negotiate a postponement of your start date, if it proves necessary to retake the exam.

But one day, the mailman is going to come, bearing your exam result. To him, its just another piece of postage. To you, its everything. The emotional roller coaster reaches its zenith with your opening up that letter. You will feel jubilation or disappointment, and there is not much in between.

If you do well on the exam, its jubilation. Congratulations on your accomplishment! Be sure to take a quiet moment to reflect on your success. You have achieved yet another milestone. Make a quick survey of the decisions you have made in the interim, while awaiting the test result. If you think it necessary or desirable to make any adjustments in those decisions, do so. One of the most important things *not* to do, however, is change your otherwise pleasant demeanor into something unbearably haughty. Its just bad form.

If you do not do well, its disappointment. At this juncture, you should assess your options and decide what is the best next move. If you were taking a professional exam on a pass/ no pass basis, you have very little choice in the matter — you have got to pass the exam to practice your chosen profession. In essence, a decision not to retake the exam is tantamount to opting for a career change, so carefully consider your decision. A non passing score is usually accompanied by a break down of your performance on the test, either by section or skill. Use this feedback as a diagnostic tool to determine where you need to improve.

If, on the other hand, the exam was not of the pass/no pass variety, but instead one on which you were trying to achieve the highest score possible, then you have the option, if time permits, to take the next administration of the exam. Know that most institutions, when interpreting the test score, will average the two exam results when considering your application. This fact should not deter you from taking the exam again, but it should cast a realistic light on how the second score will be used.

Statistically, most candidates do better on standardized tests the second time around, at least by a small margin. On some occasions, the improvement is dramatic, in which case it behooves you to do everything you can to emphasize the improved score over the disappointing one, explaining away the first score as the unusual one. Ask yourself, honestly, whether you feel in your heart that you can do better. If you gave that exam your best shot, taking it again only to achieve a lower or same score does little to advance your overall credentials. In that case, you are better off working with the score you received, and putting your fullest effort into the entire admission package. After all, as pointed out in the first chapter of this book, the exam score is but one of a number of factors that are considered by admission committees.

Success or not on the exam, do not loose perspective. It is but one component part of life, and although it may seem so, its not the most important by a long shot.

In the period of time after the exam but before the results are in, remember the following four things:

do not participate in any exam post mortem
practice some positive thinking
with respect to school and career decisions,
hope for the best and plan for the worst
do not loose perspective

101

# Conclusion

Professional examinations are here to stay. You need to master them to realize your career objectives and advance yourself in today's world. This book has shown you that mastering these exams involves test material knowledge and, just as importantly, test taking know how. By reading this book and applying some of its suggestions to your own studies, you will gain an enviable advantage over your peers. For they will learn the hard way, as they prepare for and take their exam, what you already know.

Now get to work on your preparation, and good luck to you!

# Appendix —
## Troubleshooting Guide:
### Answers to Common Concerns
### of Test Preparation

Students preparing for professional exams often have similar questions and concerns related to their test preparation. Ranging from what to do when motivation wanes to a discussion of the pros and cons of group study, this Troubleshooting Guide is designed to address some of the most universal concerns and hurdles test takers face as they prepare. Hopefully, their discussion here will limit frustration later.

**Concern:** I experience serious time problems on practice exams.

**Consider:** One of the values of practice exams is that they allow you to measure not only your grasp of concepts but of time management. If your scores are suffering because you are not completing the various sections in the time frames allotted, you must aggressively address this problem.

Start by pushing harder when you read, to read faster. You will no doubt find that your overall comprehension goes down a bit, but that may be a worthwhile tradeoff if it means you can get to more questions in the section. To get a feel for a faster pace, take a practice test, but do not correct it immediately. Instead, *retake* the test the next day, reading and answering the same questions again. Then correct it. You should find that you went through the test with greater speed the second time around. That reading speed is closer to the pace you must achieve during the actual exam. Try to take a mental measurement of that pace and apply it on the next practice exam.

The other way to address the time problem is to shorten the time in which you deliberate over the answers and make your choice. Imagine a drill sergeant hovering over you, shouting "Get in and Get out!" You get in to the question by assessing the answer choices, and then you get out of the question and on to the next one as quickly as possible. Remember that saying as you get to the answer choices. "Get in and Get out!" If the question was an easy one — a throw away for you — don't spend any time pondering it further. Just get in and get out. If the question is so complex that it has you wrapped around a pole, you have got to make the determination at some point whether to invest any further time. After a series of practice tests, you will recognize when a question starts to sap too much time. On those questions, too, you must try to get in and get out, even if you have not achieved fullest comprehension.

Diagnose which aspect of tackling the question is eating up your time: your overall reading speed, or the time you take to ponder. Use subsequent practice tests to tighten up your skills in that area. And should you find that despite diligent practice you still cannot finish the questions in the section, then use the suggestions pointed out earlier in the book: always bubble in something, choosing first those answer choices that are technically or conceptually familiar to you, and as a last resort, any answer choice at all.

**Concern**: After taking many practice tests, I notice my scores going down, not up!

**Consider**: Do not panic — declining test performance is not all that uncommon. Remember that there is only one important test score, and that is the one you achieve on the actual day of the exam. All the other ones serve you by laying the foundation of good test taking. If you find that you were doing well in a certain tested area, and now you are not doing as well as you did, take a step back and decide why.

Are you taking so many practice tests that you are burned out? If that is the problem, you might consider continuing your studies but easing up on the time constraints of practice exams. Or perhaps take a clean break from your studies altogether and give your mind a rest. In many ways, preparing for a professional exam is a lot like weight lifting at the gym. The first workout, everything is new and exciting and you give it all you've got. But if you do not give your sore muscles a couple of days to recuperate (i.e., rest), then your next gym visit will be disappointing. Similarly, you can exhaust your test preparation initiative by working at it too hard, and the result will be declining test scores. Realize that you are capable of achieving the highest test score you ever did, if not one that is higher, and any test performance that falls short of that mark is not a measure of your true abilities. You must recapture the success of the earlier performance and it may be necessary to take a break or loosen up a bit to do it.

But let's say that burn out is not your problem, that your scores are going down and you cannot figure out why. You need to do a back to basics approach to diagnose the problem. Either you have lost what is known as "section fluency," or you are in need of review of the underlying concepts and test material. Both problems can be remedied.

Section fluency refers to your familiarity and degree of comfort with the test taking format. It may be that you are rusty on the way to approach the questions in that particular test section and need to review your notes and previous tests on techniques for attacking the *question format*. For example, earlier in the book, we discussed techniques for attacking a multiple choice question for maximum time savings and comprehension. Review these suggestions if necessary. If the section involves mathematical calculations, section fluency refers to the ease with which you must diagram and solve the calculation to arrive at an answer. On essay exams, section fluency would be the suggested universal format of the essay answer, which will serve as the shell or vehicle to express your specific knowledge of the tested area. If you once did well on practice test sections involving these skills and now your scores are declining, take a moment and refresh yourself on how to efficiently and effectively deal with the question. Loss of section fluency is one of the most common culprits accounting for lower scores, but fortunately, it is also one of the most readily remedied.

If the reason your test scores are declining is that you are becoming rusty on the underlying concepts being tested, you must address the problem head on by reviewing study material which boils the information down. For example, if your exam includes science or mathematical information, review the relevant formulas, equations and definitions which form the cornerstone of so many questions. If the exam tests legal concepts or technical expertise, such as the certified public accounting or real estate licensure exam, go back and review the basic definitions and concepts. The effort will pay off.

**Concern:** Under time pressures, I get so nervous that my handwriting becomes illegible.

**Consider:** If you are taking any sort of essay or short answer exam, this seemingly unimportant issue is actually of critical importance. *If they can't read it, they can't give you credit for it.* And believe me, they will not be inclined to try. Unlike machine graded tests, exams graded by human beings are subject to human frailties (like tiredness) and emotion (like exasperation, frustration and impatience). Your exam is probably one of hundreds that a person will grade, and illegible handwriting will sour even the most pleasant mood. Why tempt the odds? Do whatever is necessary to write legibly. Try printing, if you can do so swiftly. Try slowing down when you handwrite, if that will improve things. Write on every other line to accommodate large writing or crossouts.

Some examinations allow for typewritten responses, and if you are reasonably quick with a typewriter and handwriting is a problem, give careful consideration to this option. It will involve an added hassle factor, since you will have to worry about typing under pressure. In addition, test takers who type are usually sequestered to another part of the test taking facility in order that they do not distract the handwriting crowd, so the noise level in the typing room can be deafening. But you can bring earplugs, and if typing the answer means it can be read easily, the inconvenience is worth it. If you will be typing on exam day, however, be sure to take at least half of your practice tests on a typewriter (preferably the type offered for use at the exam site) to get a feel for the time pressures while typing. Remember, too, that the typing facility offered on exam day will probably not include word processing, so get used to making manual corrections to your typewritten page. Chances are that *you* have no trouble reading your own illegible handwriting, so outline by pen what you plan to type — no sense typing that portion of the exam.

**Concern:** I'm worried about performance anxiety on test day.

**Consider:** Believe it or not, everyone is. Its just that some students have a different way than others of dealing with their anticipation and anxiety. There is no question that the testing room, the proctors, the official forms and the time constraints can be pretty intimidating to the test taker, fostering great anxiety.

There are two patterns to this anxiety. The first pattern is to experience heavy anxiety at the start of the exam, which subsides once the student is engrossed in the exam questions themselves, only to flail again if (1) the student gets stuck on a question or (2) the student has time shortages toward the end. The second pattern of anxiety is one that is constant throughout the exam period, and this pattern can be far more destructive to the student's overall exam performance.

Accept that a certain amount of anxiety is perfectly normal. If yours follows the first pattern, do what you can to concentrate on the test effort itself, and understand that the anxiety will pass once you delve into the exam. In order to stem anxiety in the event that you get stuck on a test question or run up against time constraints, review some of the test taking techniques discussed in earlier chapters. And remember that your job is not to achieve a perfect score — on many of the professional exams that is an impossibility anyway.

Your job is to do the best you can, which *is* an achievable goal.

If, on the other hand, anxiety is really getting the best of you throughout the test taking effort and exam day looms like a heart attack waiting to happen, you need to take some proactive steps to counter it. Mental exercises are often helpful. Imagine yourself taking the exam and doing really well. Follow in your mind just how you would accomplish that — your steady pace, your careful approach to the test materials and questions, and your clear thinking throughout. Review this scenario over a period of days or even weeks until it is truly familiar to you. On a smaller scale, imagine that same success in connection with each day's test preparation goals. For example, if Tuesday is the day set aside to master a certain test topic, think about the block of time you will be devoting to it, and focus on the sense of accomplishment you will feel when you have finished it. Laying the mental groundwork does wonders to stem anxiety because it gives the mind an alternative way of processing excess mental energy. Some people take all that mental concentration and walk barefoot on hot coals; all you have to do is take a dumb test!

Take any steps you can to alleviate potential anxiety. If the unfamiliarity of the test place will add to your nervousness, go there a week before the exam and just get familiar with the room and the layout of the facility. Then you can more readily imagine yourself succeeding on exam day. If the anxiety has to do with some self-doubts about your ability to show what you know, remind yourself of past accomplishments (everyone has a few, if they really consider the matter) and hold on to some of the confidence of that past. If you are distracted by what you foresee to be none other than sheer, unadulterated panic during the test itself, you must take enough of those practice tests to the point where taking the actual exam is almost like an exercise in auto pilot. Also, talk to friends and acquaintances who have already taken the exam you are taking now, and ask them about how they kept cool on exam day. They may have a good suggestion for you, and just articulating your own concern with a non-competitor (with respect to that exam, anyway) can have a therapeutic effect. You get the idea. To effectively neutralize anxiety, counter the cause.

**Concern**: My day to day study review just doesn't seem to get done — I am always too tired or have too much to do.

**Consider**: These are two different problems, leading to the same undesirable result: poor test preparation. Earlier chapters discussed how to prioritize and even how to study when you are tired. But if the problem is truly serious, not just an occasional thing, and your daily preparation effort is suffering, then you have to address some basic issues.

Firstly, like it or not, this failing is an expression of your priorities. If you can not study because you must work eighteen hours a day to put food on your table and a roof over your head, then its no wonder you are falling short with your studies. Given that type of pressure on your time and energy, you've got a valid excuse. Go into a "do it when you possibly can" mode, reviewing material when the opportunity presents itself or when you can steal away a couple hours.

That scenario is pretty extreme, however, since the great majority of those sitting for professional exams are either students, with a lot or at least a little discretionary time, or established careerists, with enough control over their work responsibilities to make time to study. If you find that competing activities get done first and all that is left for studying are your last remnants of personal strength right before you should otherwise be going to bed, make changes! Rearrange that schedule to get a good study session in, when you are most alert and refreshed. If you work all day, see if you can arrange a longer lunch break by offering to stay later in the evening. Or during the midday break, grab a quick sandwich and use the additional time to study. If you are in school, do your test review work first and class reading and school projects second. That is one way to assure that everything gets done in the day, because the class reading and school projects, no doubt, have firm deadlines which you can not ignore or put off.

Panic is a great motivator for some, so attach some urgency to your test review, if you have to. If you are always tired, and cat naps and coffee do not help, then *get more sleep*. But be twice as productive with the time you have left.

You have got to draw on everything you have to make the preparation successful, so keep making changes in your daily schedule until you figure out the best approach. When it comes to preparing for a professional exam, one all out, Herculean effort is better than having to take the whole thing again the next time around, so if nothing stirs you, that should. Those reading this book while preparing to take their exam a second or even third time are nodding their heads right now. Give it all you've got!

**Concern:** I get easily distracted when I study. Any suggestions?

**Consider:** There are two types of distractions when you study: exterior and interior. Noises, constant interruptions, even bad lighting are examples of exterior distractions. Once you identify them, do everything you can to eliminate or limit them. It may require that you study at a different place, or at a different time, or with a different group of people (if you are participating in group study, which may or may not be for you; the idea is discussed in a later problem solving section). Make special arrangements not to be disturbed,and involve your family and friends in the effort. There is nothing wrong with passing the word around that you are not available — in person or by telephone — for a certain block of time each evening. There are people who will not answer their telephone during any episode of *Jeopardy!* That's just a game show. *You* are trying to succeed on a professional exam! Be as selfish.

If, on the other hand, the distraction is interior, you have a different sort of impediment. An interior distraction is mental, and it affects your ability to concentrate on the study task at hand. For many people, the designated study time is the only time during an otherwise hectic work or school day that they have to think, so their minds wander all over the place during the time specially set aside for studying. Its a normal occurrence, but you have to do everything you can to counter it before it seriously diminishes your productivity.

The best way to end the distraction is to get focused on a particular task, the more active the better. For example, take a practice test or just do a couple of questions from a practice test to "warm up." Or use your highlighter pen to emphasize the important parts of your reading material. An earlier chapter of this book suggests ways to make your study sessions more active, and these same suggestions will help to minimize distractions, too. Lastly, if you are prone to daydreaming, then build it into the study session as a reward for good work — it doesn't cost anything, and besides, it can be a healthy release. Use it as an incentive to boost your progress, but be careful that it not take up too much of your precious study time!

If you are dogged by some problem or irritation that can be quickly and effectively addressed, try to do so in the time you have before you start studying. If, on the other hand, you are distracted by a problem that is not going to go away no matter what you can do *at this time*, then defer the worry until after the study session or after the exam! If there ever were a time to be selfish, this is it. You will have plenty of time to problem solve later, after you conquer your test.

**Concern**: I am not even sure I want to go into the field for which I am taking this exam! Its really affecting my motivation.

**Consider**: There is a certain category of test taker for whom this is a big problem. If you are taking a professional exam in order to gain a credential in your chosen field (lawyer, real estate agent, etc.), then the test is most likely the final hurdle and you have all the motivation you need. But many people take professional exams in order to gain access to certain career paths, and if they are not entirely sure of the career path at the outset, their motivation to give a professional exam their all may be hampered.

For example, to go to law school, you must take the LSAT. But you may also be planning the take the GMAT, the qualifying exam for most business schools. How well you do on either will play a part in your ultimate decision of where you may go to school and, hence, which career path you may follow. Since you are not studying for either test with set career convictions, you may have lapses in motivation. This phenomenon is common among overachievers who may be taking more than one exam, and for whom the exam is looked upon as just another academic challenge, not a career enhancer.

The trick here is to realign the objective to regain motivation. Taking the same example regarding studying for both the LSAT and GMAT, you must realign the objective to do as well on those tests as you can, in order to have as many career options as possible. Your objective becomes *creating options*, worthy of a whole lot of motivation on your part. Very few of us are born with a calling of what we would like to do with our professional lives, and many more of us simply stumble into something and before long become experts at it. If someone is studying for his or her professional test because of some childhood vision concerning that certain career, that person has all the motivation needed to keep pushing during the preparation period. But others do not approach career choices, and thus career qualifying exams, with the same fervor. If that group includes you, motivate yourself by understanding the importance of creating options. If you do really well on your exam, you will have one more avenue from which to choose in deciding the career path you will take. Do not overlook the value of choice.

It may also help to define the commitment. For goodness sakes, if you take the securities regulations exam to become a licensed stock broker, or you sit for the state licensing teachers exam, you are not necessarily signing up for those careers for life! You may go into a related area in which having that particular credential or license is a great plus. For example, consultants, writers and teachers all have a lot more credibility when they have credentials and experience in the subjects they cover. Or you may decide that you will not go into the career area at all, now that you have fully investigated it and weighed all your other options. By studying for your exam, you are merely expressing your commitment to the exam and to career options, *not* fifty years behind a desk and a gold watch for retirement — from a career you did not want anyway! See the exam for what it is, and do not drain yourself of motivation by focusing on what it is not.

**Concern**: I worry that I am over studying.

**Consider**: If you are worrying about it, you probably are. Assess your needs and your progress, and decide where you can draw the line on studying such that you are making progress and mastering the material, but also are not drowning in the effort. Over studying can lead to burnout, and when burnout strikes, productivity plummets.

There are two types of over studying. The first involves physically pushing yourself to the limit, every moment you can, to review study materials and take practice tests. You come up for air only to refuel and (sometimes) sleep. Unless that is your usual way of getting things done, do not fall into that trap while preparing for the exam. It can be physically debilitating, and is usually counterproductive anyway. Fine tune your study approach so you do not fall into that trap. Decide, objectively, what would make for adequate progress in learning the material, and stick to that study plan. Stop taking so many practice tests if you pretty much know the material and your intense drilling is causing your scores to fall.

The second type of over study is not really a case of over studying at all; it is a case of *perceived* over studying. It sets in when you fail to take a mental break from the work. In other words, even when you are not studying, you think about studying, or feel guilty about not studying, or try to study while doing something else at the same time (and, as a result, you read and reread the same sentences and stare at the same diagrams the whole time). The result? Your productivity is pretty low and you never get a break from the stuff! Deal with this problem head on by redesigning your day to include specific study periods and other times when you are absolutely off duty. No matter what you hear about friends who "never leave the library all night" or die hards who are getting perfect scores on every practice test, ignore all that and structure your study day for *your* maximum efficiency. Include time to recharge your batteries and refresh yourself. Its the only way to fight burnout caused by perceived over study.

**Concern:** This is not the first time that I have taken the exam; my last try was a disappointment, and I am having motivation problems now.

**Consider:** First off, you deserve high praise for having the drive to take the exam again. Not everyone picks themselves up, brushes themselves off, and gets back in the saddle. You are doing that, and you are showing what you are made of by doing so. Your circumstances are indeed unique, in that you have done it all before, and probably put in a lot of effort when you did. It is perfectly normal to have lapses of motivation the second (or even third) time around. You worry that once again your effort might not pay off.

But consider your advantages! You have taken the exam before, under real exam conditions, and you know what to expect on exam day. That is an enviable advantage in countering anxiety. And statistically, test takers achieve better scores on second and even third test administrations. That familiarity is going to work for you, too.

The other advantage you have, having gone through the test preparation process before, is knowing what does and does not work for you. Be honest with yourself. Assess your last preparation effort. Were there things you know you should have done differently to prepare? Did you get the most out of your study sessions? Were there specific aspects of the exam for which you felt less prepared? By analyzing your last effort, you can substantially improve the current one. If your last exam results came with some sort of score breakdown, you can use that information to design an even more effective study approach. While still reviewing all the basic material, emphasize review of those areas which gave you the most trouble on the previous exam. That could be a certain body of knowledge related to your field and therefore tested on the exam, or problem solving approaches which you need to better commit to memory. Whatever it is, you are uniquely positioned to make your next study effort exceptionally well targeted, and you should do so.

When you meet fellow test takers, no one has to know that you are taking the exam again, unless you choose to tell them. If it makes you the slightest bit uncomfortable, just don't mention it. As for family, friends, classmates or coworkers who may know that you are taking it again, show them the right attitude and you will be surprised by their support of your efforts. The right attitude is one of self-respect and dedication to your own success. If you are down and self-effacing about it all, they will pick up on that, too.

Because attitude and motivation play such a key role in your study efforts, you have got to look upon your circumstance as a hidden advantage. That earlier exam laid the groundwork for your success now!

**Concern**: In addition to studying for the exam, I am preparing applications for admission to graduate school. The process feels overwhelming.

**Consider**: That's understandable. Between the stress of the exam *and* applications, things can get a little overwhelming.

Sometimes the sheer magnitude of the project induces a kind of paralysis, where you can not get much of anything done, and as a result of that, the project becomes even more daunting.

The trick here is to break it all down into component parts. Accomplish one of those components each day, no matter how small it may seem to you. On the graduate school application front, make a list of all the things you will need to do to prepare the application package, and make some headway on at least one of those items each day. For example, one day's progress may be just obtaining the necessary forms to order transcripts from your college. Another day, outline the answer to an essay question or work on your biographical statement. Just do something each day to move yourself closer to completing the whole process. The component parts will not overwhelm you, and you will enjoy the feeling that you are making progress each day. This approach works best when you have a good bit of time to do all you have to do, such as sixty or ninety days. If you are faced with shorter deadlines, or you are starting late, then just accelerate your pace in accomplishing the component list. The quality of your finished applications will benefit from this gradualist approach, and it will do wonders to control your anxiety over the whole process.

**Concern:** I started to prepare for my exam too late. Are there ways to streamline preparation?

**Consider:** There's too late and then there is *really* too late. You know its *really* too late if you're just starting to review material less than a week before the exam. In that case, use whatever time you may have to *acquaint yourself with the format of the exam.* Anything you can do above and beyond that, like take a practice test or two, is a plus. Believe it or not, there are those who just show up on exam day with no more than that little preparation, and some do quite well. Of course, those people annoy the hell out of the rest of us, but as long as we get our chance to shine, too, it really does not matter.

For some test takers, it is difficult to set aside the hours or get organized enough to sustain the study priority over a long period of time. As a result, their preparation efforts do not gain any momentum until the last month or so. This pattern is actually quite typical, and it can work to your advantage if it leads you to "peak" on exam day.

If you feel that you are getting a late start on preparation, structure the time left with the following four priorities in mind: First, as previously mentioned, you must fully acquaint yourself with the format of the exam. Be familiar with what is tested and how it will be tested. Look at past exams or informational material sent by the test maker, and get a complete understanding for the directions on each section of the exam. This step is crucial, because you must first understand *how* to show what you know.

Next, determine if any part of the test will involve problem solving *techniques* instead of or in addition to basic knowledge of the field. If so, spend some time on that. For example, many professional exams, especially those used for graduate school admission purposes, will include "logic games" or math sections that will ask you to reach a solution by employing certain problem solving techniques (diagramming, process of elimination, solving by analogy, etc.). Understand how to approach these questions.

If you are taking any kind of professional *licensing* exam, the third priority is to review the underlying material to be tested. Spend some time studying the definitions, theories, laws, and policies that may be on the exam.

Lastly, no matter what kind of exam it is, take practice tests. They will give you an instant measure of how you are doing and also give you a feel for the time restrictions.

Take these priorities and figure in how much time you have to prepare. Make a study schedule and stick to it. Some exam preparation companies offer "express review" courses for the late starter. If such a course would give you some needed structure, strongly consider signing up.

Above all, keep your cool. You do not need to start studying a year in advance to do exceptionally well on a professional exam. If you feel you are getting a late start, effectively use the time you do have to study. By keeping your cool, you will maintain your sense of self-confidence on exam day.

**Concern**: I am not sure if I should join a study group.

**Consider**: In preparation for a professional licensing exam, students sometimes form a study group to review and discuss substantive material. There are distinct pros and cons to joining such a group. Here are the things to consider:

First, if your test is not a licensing exam but instead is a graduate admission exam, you will probably do much better with your time to study alone. Those exams emphasize certain test taking skills that you acquire through diligent self-study (practice tests, techniques, time drills, etc.). Study groups, on the other hand, are most effectively used for learning and understanding the underlying material to be tested. On a licensing exam, that could include certain definitions, laws, professional rules and other substantive material which you must commit to memory. A study group can help you do that, especially if there are aspects to the material that you do not yet understand or that you forgot over time. Study group discussion stimulates memory, and you have an additional resource in your study group for understanding difficult material. Explaining to others something that you know is another advantage, because doing so will cement further your own understanding.

But group study can have its disadvantages, too. Groups of more than four people soon become counterproductive. Group meetings lasting more than two hours do too. Often, a group meeting deteriorates into a group panic session, and there is no benefit in that. If the group is not comprised of equally motivated students, the study sessions will suffer. Lastly, study groups *can not* take the place of solitary study and practice test taking. At best, a study group *supplements* your own efforts. Why not just try a session or two, without committing, if you can.

With those warnings made, some students swear by study groups and find an added benefit in the comraderie they foster. After all, no one better understands the pressure of preparing for a professional exam than another who is.

**Concern**: I am taking my professional exam for the second time and hope to do considerably better. How do I "explain away" my earlier score?

**Consider**: If you are taking a professional licensing exam, there will be no need to explain your earlier attempt. The most important fact will be whether you have passed at all, and you plan to pass this time! Close colleagues, family and friends should recognize your dedication to your field and applaud your efforts. Professional acquaintances you meet in the future will not even know.

If, however, you did poorly on a numerically scored exam and are wondering how to best emphasize to an admissions committee a more recent, improved score, that then is an entirely different issue. In that case, you do not want to hide it at all, but instead highlight the improvement with reference to it somewhere on your application materials.

Perhaps you were physically sick when you took the exam for the first time, or there were certain other circumstances that prevented you from reaching peak performance on test day. Do not invent an excuse, but if there are relevant outside details that will allow an admissions committee to better understand the meaning of your scores, tell them. If the difference in performance is mainly due to hard work and plain old improvement on your part, be honest and explain that, too. Perhaps the earlier, disappointing score was your wake up call, and the higher score is more fairly representative of what you can achieve. Turn the improvement to your advantage in order to give the higher score the best possible spin.

# ABOUT THE AUTHOR

*Survival Guide to Professional Exams — Preparation Tips to Ace the Test!* was written by **Michael Africk**, an attorney credentialed in California and Illinois. Along the way, he has taken quite a few of the professional exams discussed in the book, and has taught graduate admission test review courses for both the LSAT (Law School Admission Test) and GMAT (Graduate Management Admission Test). This book is written from his personal experience in test taking and teaching.

Got any preparation tips to pass along?

For comments, questions and ordering information, contact:

Bentley Press
P.O. Box 3084- D
Peoria, Illinois 61612-3084

# NOTES

# NOTES